D0621030

TEEAL

ENERGY
SECURITY

Essential Issues

ENERGY SECURITY

BY HAL MARCOVITZ

Content Consultant
Fred Yarger, PhD
Independent Energy Consultant

3 1336 08710 0302

ABDO
Publishing Company

SAN DIEGO PUBLIC LIBRARY
TEEN SPACE

CREDITS

Published by ABDO Publishing Company, 8000 West 78th Street, Edina, Minnesota 55439. Copyright © 2011 by Abdo Consulting Group, Inc. International copyrights reserved in all countries. No part of this book may be reproduced in any form without written permission from the publisher. The Essential Library™ is a trademark and logo of ABDO Publishing Company.

Printed in the United States of America,
North Mankato, Minnesota
112010
012011

 THIS BOOK CONTAINS AT LEAST 10% RECYCLED MATERIALS.

Editor: Melissa Johnson
Copy Editor: Amy E. Quale
Interior Design and Production: Marie Tupy
Cover Design: Marie Tupy

Library of Congress Cataloging-in-Publication Data
Marcovitz, Hal.
  Energy security / by Hal Marcovitz.
    p. cm. -- (Essential issues)
  Includes bibliographical references.
  ISBN 978-1-61714-771-5
  1. Petroleum reserves--Juvenile literature. 2. Energy consumption--Juvenile literature. 3. Energy development--Juvenile literature. 4. Energy industries--Juvenile literature. I. Title.
  HD9560.5.M3125 2011
  333.79--dc22

                                        2010041256

TABLE OF CONTENTS

Many oil tankers pass through the Strait of Hormuz in the Persian Gulf.

THE STRAIT OF HORMUZ

The confrontation had a foregone conclusion. Five small patrol boats manned by sailors of the Iranian Navy approached three huge US Navy vessels, including the guided missile destroyer USS *Hopper*. The five boats swerved in and out of the paths of the US Navy ships while over the radio the Iranians issued a defiant warning: "You will explode after a few minutes!"[1]

The incident, which occurred on January 6, 2008, was over after about 20 minutes. As the sailors aboard the US Navy vessels took aim, the tiny Iranian boats finally sped away. No shots were fired. There is no question, however, that if the order had been given, the Americans would have blasted the Iranian boats out of the water in seconds.

Iran and the United States have been unfriendly since 1979 when Islamic militants toppled a US-backed government in that country. US officials were alarmed by the 2008 incident, even though the five tiny patrol boats were no real threat to the larger US ships. In Washington DC, President George W. Bush issued some harsh words about the incident: "We viewed it as a

On the Verge of Firing

According to US military officials, one of the ships confronted by the Iranian patrol boats on January 6, 2008, came within seconds of firing. An Iranian patrol boat sailed to within 200 yards (183 m) of USS *Hopper*, a guided missile destroyer. As the boat approached, the US ship broadcast this warning: "You are approaching a coalition warship operating in international waters. Your identity is not known. Your intentions are unclear."[2] The commanding officer of the *Hopper* was on the verge of giving the firing order when the Iranian boat suddenly steered clear.

provocative act. It is a dangerous situation, and they should not have done it, pure and simple."[3]

The situation was dangerous because it occurred at the entrance of the Persian Gulf in a narrow waterway known as the Strait of Hormuz. The strait serves as the main route for tankers transporting crude oil from Saudi Arabia, Kuwait, and other Middle Eastern oil producers to refineries in Europe, Asia, South America, and the United States. Some 20 percent of the world's oil supply passes through the strait, which is only 21 miles (34 km) wide at its narrowest point. The US Navy maintains a heavy presence in the strait, guaranteeing that the tankers have safe passage.

Protecting the Tankers

Iran borders the Persian Gulf, including the Strait of Hormuz. The US military must ensure the flow of oil through the strait in order to maintain the energy security of the United States and its allies. The confrontation shows how seriously the US government regards its mission to protect the tankers. If the Iranians ever interrupt the oil shipments, the economies of the United States and many other countries could be thrown into chaos.

Suddenly cutting off 20 percent of the world's oil supply would cause fuel prices to skyrocket in many areas. If the supply were cut off for an extended period of time, shortages of gasoline, diesel fuel, and heating oil could occur. Commerce might slow if trucking companies were to have trouble fueling their trucks to transport goods. Oil rationing might begin.

To prevent such a disruption, experts believe the United States would not hesitate to use its military might against Iran. Said Michael T.

How Important Is the Persian Gulf?

In 2009, 1.7 million barrels of crude oil were shipped through the Persian Gulf to the United States each day. This number was expected to grow to 3.5 million barrels a day for all of North America by 2030, as estimated in 2007 by the Washington DC–based Center for Strategic and International Studies, which examines national security issues.

A barrel contains 42 gallons (159 L) of crude oil. According to the US Department of Energy, US refineries produce approximately 20 gallons (76 L) of gasoline from a single barrel. (The remainder of the barrel makes other fuels and products.) In one day, the oil shipped through the Strait of Hormuz produces approximately 50 million gallons (189 million L) of gasoline.

That is a significant amount of gasoline, but Americans use much more than that. The Energy Department estimates that US cars consume 375 million gallons (1.4 billion L) of gasoline every day. Middle East oil is supplemented by oil produced in oil-rich states and offshore platforms in the Gulf of Mexico and by other oil exporters, including Canada, Mexico, Venezuela, and Nigeria. In 2009, the United States imported more oil from Canada (approximately 900 million barrels) than from the Persian Gulf countries combined (approximately 620 million barrels).

Klare, a political science professor at Hampshire College in Massachusetts and an expert on energy issues:

> *The United States would greet any Iranian move to impede Persian Gulf shipping with an immediate and crushing military response. . . . And while the Iranians might succeed in damaging a number of tankers, their ability to imperil the oil flow would quickly be eliminated by superior American firepower.*[4]

OPERATION BRIMSTONE

Seven months after the confrontation, the US military launched Operation Brimstone. US Navy warships, including the aircraft carrier USS *Theodore Roosevelt*, began a training exercise in the Atlantic Ocean designed to simulate conditions in the Strait of Hormuz. Joining the US vessels in Operation Brimstone were ships from Great Britain, France, and Brazil—all

An Alternate Route

If the Strait of Hormuz were closed to shipping, the Middle Eastern oil-producing nations would have an alternate route for exporting their crude: a 745-mile (1,199-km) pipeline that crosses Saudi Arabia and ends at the Red Sea. From there, the oil could be shipped north through the Suez Canal into the Mediterranean Sea or south through the Gulf of Aden into the Indian Ocean. That pipeline can move about 5 million barrels a day, or about 20 percent of the oil shipped through the Persian Gulf. Experts believe that if the Strait of Hormuz were blocked and the Middle Eastern oil producers found themselves relying on an overland pipeline, the price of oil would skyrocket.

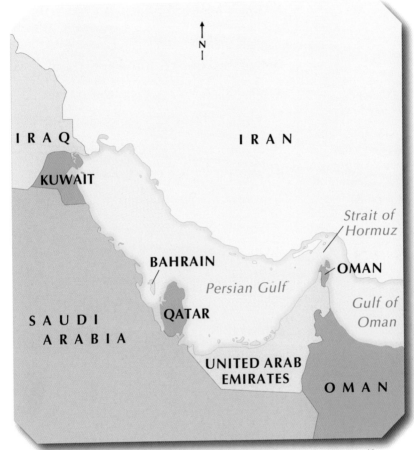

The Strait of Hormuz is located at the entrance to the Persian Gulf in the Middle East.

countries that purchase oil from the Persian Gulf region.

During Operation Brimstone, ships cruised back and forth while fighter planes launched from the deck of the *Theodore Roosevelt* zoomed overhead.

"The World Came Very Close to War"

Walter Russell Mead is a senior fellow at the Council on Foreign Relations, a New York City–based organization that studies international issues. He said the United States would have been within its rights to attack Iran following the January 6, 2008, confrontation between the Iranian and US navies. "The world came very close to war on Sunday," Mead said. "The Straits of Hormuz, site of the weekend provocation, are exceptionally sensitive. The ability of the US to protect the free flow of oil through these waters is absolutely vital to the global economy. Any US military response to a challenge there would be swift and overwhelming—perhaps far greater than the Iranians expect."[6]

Military leaders described Operation Brimstone as a training exercise, but there is no question the event was intended to send a message to the Iranians: Harassment of US military ships or commercial oil tankers would not be tolerated. As for the Iranians, they remained defiant. "If the enemy goes insane, we will drown them . . . before they reach the Strait of Hormuz and the entrance to the Persian Gulf," insisted Iranian Navy Admiral Habibollah Sayyari shortly after the conclusion of Operation Brimstone.[5]

Since the January 2008 confrontation in the Persian Gulf, Iran has found itself facing internal turmoil as many citizens began protesting the government, demanding an end to the country's authoritarian rule. Many of the protestors in Iran have also demanded better relations with the United States. The Iranian leaders

This tiny boat approached the USS Hopper *on January 6, 2008.*

have reacted harshly, dispatching police into the streets to crack down on protesters. Meanwhile, some believe the Iranian government is trying to develop nuclear weapons. Leaders in the United States and elsewhere fear what could happen if such destructive weapons fell into the hands of a hostile regime.

If Iran were to make another hostile move against the United States or its allies, chances are a confrontation would occur in the Persian Gulf. That is why the United States maintains a strong military presence in the Gulf, guarding the tiny strait that has an enormous influence over the energy security of the United States and its allies.

The USS Hopper, shown here in San Francisco, was threatened
in the Strait of Hormuz in 2008.

Cities need lots of energy to keep lights shining and people moving.

THE IMPORTANCE OF ENERGY SECURITY

The US economy and all other modern world economies depend on energy. Oil, natural gas, coal, wind, sun, and nuclear power all provide the energy that keeps people warm in their homes, keeps cars and trucks running, and keeps industries operating and productive. For modern industrial societies, any interruption to the flow of energy has usually had disastrous consequences, including high unemployment, food shortages, and freezing winters. "A reliable energy supply is one of the basic prerequisites for a functioning economy," explained Sascha Müller-Kraenner, an analyst for the Ecologic Institute, a Washington DC organization that studies environmental issues.[1]

This fact was as true a century ago as it is today. In 1914, on the brink of World War I, Winston Churchill, the future prime minister of Great Britain, was head of the Royal Navy. He ordered all British warships to be converted from coal power to oil power. Churchill knew the production of coal would slow down in time of war. He also knew Britain had a strong military presence in the Middle East. With this, he could

Coal Shortage Led to German Defeat

In 1920, the economist Kurt Königsberger studied what led to the German defeat in World War I. Wrote Königsberger, "Whoever had the opportunity to study the papers of the [German] authorities would be struck again and again in all letters and reports, telegrams and notices, by the words: coal shortage!"[2]

guarantee oil would be delivered to Great Britain and its allies. Great Britain's enemy Germany continued to rely on coal. Soon, as Churchill predicted, less coal was mined and supply lines were interrupted by warfare. Germany was unable to supply energy to its army and navy as well as its citizens. By the end of the war in 1918, Germany was almost out of coal.

UNFRIENDLY REGIMES

Since the Industrial Revolution began in the nineteenth century, energy has been vital to industrialized societies. According to the US Department of Energy, global demand for energy increased by nearly 50 percent between 1980 and 2003. It is projected to increase by another 33 percent from 2010 through 2030. In 2009, US cars and trucks used 140 billion gallons (529 billion L) of gasoline, as well as 45 billion gallons (170 billion L) of diesel fuel. Although oil wells, pipelines, and refineries dot the US landscape, the United States imported 53 percent of its oil in 2009. Some of that oil is imported from countries with unstable regimes or countries that are openly unfriendly to US interests, such as Venezuela and Libya.

Venezuelans marched in protest against US President George W. Bush on May 1, 2006. The sign reads, "No to Imperialism."

Hugo Chavez, the president of Venezuela, has given hostile speeches against the United States. He once compared former President George W. Bush to the devil. "The devil came here yesterday," Chavez said in 2006 from the podium of the United Nations (UN), which Bush had addressed the day before, "and it smells of sulfur still today."[3]

In 2009, Venezuela shipped more than 1 million barrels of oil to the United States each day. With such an unfriendly regime in power, however, US officials are understandably concerned. If President Chavez were to decide to cut off the flow of Venezuelan oil to the United States, US consumers would likely see a rise in the price of gasoline and other petroleum products and might even face shortages.

Another longtime enemy of the United States, Libyan leader Mu'ammar al-Gadhafi, has been considered a supporter of international terrorism. Libya has admitted to backing the terrorists who planted a bomb aboard a US commercial airliner in 1988; the bomb exploded over Lockerbie, Scotland, killing 270 people. The bombing led to an international censure of Libya. Many countries refused to buy Libyan oil after the

Cheap Oil from Venezuela

Venezuelan President Hugo Chavez has been a harsh critic of the United States, but he has also authorized the sale of Venezuelan oil at a deep discount to organizations that supply heating oil to low-income Americans. "We'll continue to support a people whose government is hostile to us," insisted Bernardo Alvarez, the Venezuelan ambassador to the United States. "We have nothing against this country."[4]

Libya's leader, Mu'ammar al-Gadhafi. The United States buys oil from several unfriendly countries, including Libya.

attack. Only after Gadhafi renounced terrorism in 2002 and agreed to pay nearly $3 billion to the families of the dead passengers did the United States resume buying oil from Libya. Still, Gadhafi's regime is hostile to the United States and its allies.

Even some friendlier oil exporters raise concerns. Saudi Arabia is a dedicated US ally in the Middle East, but human rights activists have criticized its rulers. In the face of these concerns, US diplomats must maintain delicate relations with oil-producing nations. Sometimes, they must work with undemocratic governments or ignore human rights abuses.

Riots in New York

Energy security goes beyond keeping friendly relations with foreign powers or using military power to guarantee the safety of oil

Human Rights in Saudi Arabia

The United States maintains friendly relations with the Saudis, but US officials acknowledge cases in which the kingdom has violated human rights. A US State Department report explained:

Principal human rights issues include abuse of prisoners and [silent] detention; prohibitions or severe restrictions on freedom of speech, press, peaceful assembly and association, and religion; denial of the right of citizens to change their government; systematic discrimination against women and ethnic and religious minorities; and suppression of workers' rights.[5]

According to the human rights group Amnesty International, Saudi law permits offenders to be put to death by beheading. Saudis face mutilation, flogging, or the death penalty for acts such as theft, adultery, blasphemy, witchcraft, and the sale or consumption of drugs and alcohol.

Amnesty International estimates that at least 100 people were executed in Saudi Arabia in 2008, some by beheading. The organization also reported that people who committed their crimes when they were minors were among those executed.

tankers. Americans have often discovered that when the flow of energy is interrupted at home, chaos results. That is what happened in 1977 when on the sweltering night of July 13, a series of lightning strikes set off a chain of events that shut off power in New York City for 25 hours.

At first, New Yorkers faced the blackout with a resolve to carry on their lives as usual. On Broadway, actors played their roles and stagehands shined flashlights onto the stages. Waiters served meals by candlelight. Mayor Abraham Beame tried to keep his sense of humor. "See? This is what you get for not paying your bills," he quipped.[6]

The joke was soon over when vandals and looters took over the streets, causing tens of millions of dollars in damage. At one automobile dealership in the city, vandals smashed through the windows and

"A War Out Here"

One of the witnesses to the New York City rioting of 1977 was Miguel Ten, a Vietnam War veteran and a security guard at a children's clothing store. Nearby, looters had broken into Hearn's, a department store. They stripped clothing from mannequins, then broke the mannequins apart and threw them into the street. Surveying the scene, Ten said, "This reminds me of [Vietnam] in 1966. There was a war out here. And the mannequins remind me of the dead people I saw in Nam without legs and arms."[7]

stole 50 cars. Thieves broke into grocery stores, filling shopping bags with food. After the lights came back on, fire officials reported that city firefighters fought 1,037 blazes during the previous night, all started intentionally.

Clearly, as the New York City riots illustrate, when the smooth supply of energy breaks down, the social order can break down as well. Blackouts do not always cause riots, but blackouts can trigger riots when other underlying conditions are right, such as poverty or social unrest. That is why US officials must be vigilant in ensuring that energy continues to flow without interruption. The heads of hostile foreign powers know this as well, and it is likely that they will continue to test the ability of the United States to provide energy to its citizens.

Passersby examine the aftereffects of the looting during the New York blackout in 1977.

*Israeli forces were victorious in the Yom Kippur War in the 1970s,
one conflict of many that have taken place in the Middle East.*

RARELY SAFE, CHEAP,
AND RELIABLE

On October 6, 1973, Egypt and Syria launched an attack on Israel to regain territory the two Arab nations lost in an earlier conflict. The attack on the predominately Jewish country began on Yom Kippur, the holiest day on the Jewish calendar. At first, the Arab armies made advances. But they were soon repelled by Israeli forces, who received weapons from the US government and several European allies. Ultimately, the Yom Kippur War ended in an Israeli victory.

Egypt and Syria were backed by Saudi Arabia and other Middle Eastern oil-producing states. To punish the United States and the European nations for their support for Israel, the Saudis and other Middle Eastern states declared an embargo on oil shipments that lasted for six months. It ended when US Secretary of State Henry Kissinger was able to negotiate an Israeli withdrawal from Arab territories.

In the meantime, Americans and many Europeans learned a harsh lesson about energy security. During the embargo, motorists were forced to wait in long lines to fill up their cars while gasoline prices soared.

Grim Prediction

In the 1940s, US Interior Secretary Harold Ickes predicted that the United States would have to rely on other countries to provide oil and that without oil, the United States would not be able to maintain its own security. "If there should be a World War III," Ickes warned, "it would have to be fought with someone else's petroleum."[1]

For years, gasoline had cost pennies and always seemed plentiful. In the 1970s, Americans were appalled when gasoline prices rose higher than $1 per gallon (3.8 L). In Great Britain, government officials pleaded with their citizens to use less energy—to turn lights off when not in use, to refrain from driving unnecessarily, and to turn the heat down in their homes. Said British Prime Minister Edward Heath, "We shall have a harder Christmas than we have known since [World War II]."[2]

Instability in the Middle East

Since the embargo of 1973–1974, other international incidents have driven up the price of gasoline, heating oil, and other petroleum products. In 1979, a group of Islamic extremists overthrew Iran's leader, Shah Mohammad Reza Pahlavi, who had governed since 1953. The shah had been a close ally of US oil interests, guaranteeing delivery of his country's vast petroleum

Invading Saudi Arabia

When the Saudis and other Middle East oil exporters declared the oil embargo in 1973, President Richard M. Nixon considered launching a US invasion of the kingdom in order to take over the country's oil reserves. Nixon consulted with Secretary of State Henry Kissinger, who convinced Nixon that the region would become too unstable to control following an invasion and that this would cause even higher oil prices. In the years following the embargo, the icy relations between the United States and Saudi Arabia have warmed.

reserves to US consumers. His overthrow in 1979 led to the establishment of a strongly anti-United States regime in Iran that has remained in power into the twenty-first century. Following the overthrow of the shah, Iranian oil exports to the United States ceased. Within a year, oil prices on the world market doubled as the other oil-producing nations raised their prices and profited from the crisis.

Over the years, the Middle East has remained one of the most politically unstable regions on the planet. That instability is often sparked by disputes over the sales of oil. During the 1980s, Iraqi dictator Saddam Hussein waged a long and bloody war against neighboring Iran. The war ended in a stalemate. However, the conflict cost Iraq billions of dollars. Hussein was desperate for money as oil prices remained low. He blamed his country's southern neighbor, Kuwait. Kuwait had lent Iraq a lot of money during the war, and it was now demanding repayment. The Iraqi dictator also accused the Kuwaitis of making too much oil available on the world market, thus driving down prices. On August 2, 1990, Iraq launched an invasion of Kuwait.

A partnership of armies led by the United States quickly mobilized. After months of negotiations

Kuwaiti oil wells were set on fire during the Persian Gulf War in 1991.

failed to convince Hussein to withdraw his troops, a
US-led invasion of Iraq and Kuwait began in early
1991. The Persian Gulf War was over in a matter

of weeks as the United States and its allies defeated the Iraqi forces. Near the conclusion of the war, as the Iraqis fled Kuwait, they set fire to the Kuwaiti oil wells. Oil fire experts from Texas were quickly rushed to the scene, but it took months to extinguish the blazes.

When the Iraqis invaded Kuwait, the situation unsettled world oil markets and the price of crude oil rose. Prices remained high for months after the war, until the fires were extinguished and the Kuwaitis resumed pumping oil.

ENVIRONMENTAL HAZARDS

Energy security is a wide-ranging issue that covers more than just US military or diplomatic responses to crises in the Middle East. According to the International Energy Agency, an organization that monitors worldwide energy use, energy security is having "reasonably priced, reliable, and environmentally friendly energy."[3] Over the years, there have been numerous cases in which energy production has posed a threat to the environment. In 1989, the huge oil tanker *Exxon Valdez* struck a reef in Prince William Sound in Alaska, spilling 11 million gallons (42 million L) of crude oil.

Exxon Valdez Crude Continues to Pollute

A 2006 study found that traces of crude oil spilled during the 1989 *Exxon Valdez* accident continue to affect wildlife habitats. Birds and aquatic mammals such as otters are still consuming the oil. Said research chemist Jeffrey Short, who published his findings in the journal *Environmental Science & Technology*, "This study shows that it is very plausible that exposure to *Exxon Valdez* oil is having a material impact on many shore-dwelling animals and is contributing to their slow recovery in some parts of Prince William Sound."[4]

The mucky crude seemed to spread everywhere, coating the rocky shoreline and fouling wildlife habitats. Two decades after the spill, evidence suggests contamination still affects wildlife in Prince William Sound.

On December 22, 2008, a spill of 1 billion gallons (3.8 billion L) of liquefied coal ash from the Kingston Fossil Plant swamped the community of Kingston, Tennessee, driving many residents out of their homes. Coal ash is a byproduct of coal combustion, left over after the fuel is burned in plants that make electricity. It contains many toxic ingredients, including mercury, arsenic, and lead. For decades, the Tennessee Valley Authority, which owns the plant, had dumped the ash into a pond adjacent to the Emory River. In 2008, the pond's earthen walls collapsed, swamping the town. The US Environmental Protection

Agency (EPA) trucked tons of the liquefied ash out of town, but Kingston residents remained concerned about returning home. "The breathing is what concerns me, the lung issues," said Kingston resident Angela Spurgeon, a mother of two young children. "Who knows what's in that water?"[5]

GULF OF MEXICO OIL SPILL

On April 20, 2010, an explosion and a fire occurred on an oil rig in the Gulf of Mexico. The explosion killed 11 workers. The rig, known as Deepwater Horizon, sunk into the ocean within a few days. At first, observers saw no oil spilling. Within days, however, a leak was discovered. Early attempts

The Town That Went Away

In 1962, a trash fire spread to a coal mine that snaked beneath the Pennsylvania town of Centralia. The hard-packed coal in the mine caught fire. No one has ever been able to put out the fire.

For years, the people of Centralia lived above the fire, but by the 1980s smoke containing toxic fumes started escaping through large cracks that had opened up in the streets and surrounding terrain. Before the fire, 1,400 people lived in Centralia. Most people left town after the federal government bought and razed their homes.

Fewer than a dozen people live in the town's last remaining homes. Somehow they manage to avoid the high levels of toxic carbon monoxide that seep out of the ground. They also avoid being swallowed up by the cracks that open up from time to time in the town's loose soil. "I busy myself trying to take care of the grounds," said longtime resident John Lokitis. "Trying to keep it like the street that time forgot."[6]

to cap the well were unsuccessful and crews could not stop the flow of oil. Estimates of the volume of the leak continued to rise in the subsequent weeks as the first oil rolled ashore in Louisiana and then Alabama, eventually reaching as far away as Florida. Throughout the disaster, crews worked to clean up as much oil as possible. By July, federal government estimates of 140 million gallons (530 million L) spilled made it the largest oil spill ever in the Gulf of Mexico. By mid-July, a new cap on the well was holding.

The spill was considered by many to be among the worst environmental disasters in US history. Besides the visible damage to animals and ecosystems, the spill also caused much economic damage, harming the livelihoods of the people of the Gulf Coast who relied on fishing and tourism for their incomes. Scientists will continue to monitor the Gulf's plants and animals for years to measure the impact the spill had on the environment.

A shrimp boat was used to collect oil after the April 20 oil rig explosion in the Gulf of Mexico in May 2010.

Energy infrastructure such as oil pipelines might be vulnerable to terrorist attacks.

Terrorism and Piracy

The winter of 2006 was particularly harsh for the residents of Tbilisi, the capital of Georgia, in eastern Europe. In January, terrorists exploded bombs that destroyed the pipelines supplying natural gas to the capital. A main electric transmission line was also blown up by a bomb. For several days, homes, schools, and businesses lacked heat. Factories came to a standstill. In the streets, long lines formed as people waited for kerosene and firewood to provide temporary heat. In the midst of the crisis, Georgian officials signed a hasty deal with the Iranian government to provide emergency gas while the main supply lines were repaired.

The Georgians never found out who bombed their pipelines, but there was no lack of suspects. Some Georgian officials suspected it was the work of Islamic extremists. Others believed the terrorism had its roots in a dispute between the Georgian government and Gazprom, the national gas company of Russia that sells Georgia its natural gas supplies. Gazprom informed Georgia that it planned to raise prices, but Georgian officials balked at paying the higher rates. Georgian President Mikheil Saakashvili accused the Russians of ordering the attack. "We don't think this is accidental in any

Winters in Georgia

Winters are usually mild in the Republic of Georgia, but the terrorists who targeted the country's gas and electric lines waited for a cold snap to hit the country. Not only did people have to suffer in their unheated homes, but they had to line up outside in bitterly cold temperatures for emergency supplies of kerosene and firewood. "The electricity went off at one in the morning and since then we've been freezing," said Irakli Gogokhidze, an elderly Georgian forced to wait in freezing temperatures for his share of kerosene.[1]

The Trans-Alaska Pipeline

A Canadian man was sentenced to 13 years in prison in 2008 after pleading guilty to a plot to blow up the Trans-Alaska Pipeline, which funnels approximately 14 percent of the oil produced in the United States over an 800-mile (1,287-km) course across Alaska. Alfred Heinz Reumayr said he had no political motive for the bombing but had invested in oil and wished to drive up the price of crude by disrupting supplies to the United States.

way," Saakashvili said. "The places where it happened, the environment in which it happened, the history in which it happened—this all looks like a policy decision."[2] Russian officials quickly dismissed the charge. Two years later, hostilities between Georgia and Russia grew worse, causing the Russian army to briefly invade Georgia.

TERRORISM AND NUCLEAR PLANTS

The attack on Georgia's pipelines illustrates how vulnerable energy supplies can be to terrorism. Terrorists know if they knock out a power plant or oil refinery, they can cause many problems for their targets. Explained energy security experts Gal Luft and Anne Korin:

> *Terrorist organizations have always been interested in targeting oil and gas facilities. Striking pipelines, tankers, refineries, and oil fields accomplishes two desired goals: Undermining the internal stability of the regimes they are fighting, and economically weakening foreign powers with vested interests in their region.[3]*

In the days following the September 11, 2001, terrorist attacks on the World Trade Center and the Pentagon, US government officials realized the widespread damage that could have happened if the terrorists had targeted nuclear power plants, gas lines, or oil refineries. Soon after the 2001 attacks, the US Nuclear Regulatory Commission (NRC) ordered all 65 nuclear plants in the United States to improve their security systems.

Still, the NRC has concluded that nuclear plants, by their nature, are built to withstand natural disasters and even terrorism.

Trouble in Ecuador

The discovery of oil deep in the Amazon jungle in Ecuador has brought in billions of dollars for the country. However, little of that money has helped ordinary Ecuadorians. In August 2005, hundreds of protesters organized by the Confederation of Indigenous Nationalities of Ecuador took over Ecuador's oil fields. The protesters shut down oil production in the South American country for about a week.

They demanded the Ecuadoran government spend its oil profits on building new roads and providing jobs to poor people. During the week the protesters controlled the country's oil fields, they stopped the production of more than 1 million barrels of oil. All of that oil would have been shipped to the United States.

The government finally sent in troops to drive the protesters out of the oil fields. After taking back control, government leaders found widespread damage. Repairs took months. "What happened is worse than war," said Ivan Rodriguez, Ecuador's oil minister.[4] Despite the damage, government officials promised that more of the country's oil money would be used to improve life for ordinary Ecuadorians. Those changes have been slow to materialize, though, and the Confederation has since staged many protests in the streets of Quito, Ecuador's capital.

Engineers take many precautions to avoid exposing
the dangerous radioactive reactor core. Explained
the Nuclear Energy Institute, a trade association:

> Steel-reinforced concrete containment structures are
> designed to withstand the impact of hurricanes, tornadoes,
> earthquakes, and floods, as well as airborne objects with a
> substantial force.[5]

THE THREAT OF PIRACY

Meanwhile, a new threat to energy security has
surfaced in recent years. Off the coast of Somalia
in East Africa, hundreds of modern-day pirates
began attacking shipping routes in the Indian
Ocean in the 1990s. They seized ships, including
oil tankers, holding the vessels and their crews for
ransom. A shocking attack occurred in 2008 when
four pirates seized the Saudi Arabian SS *Sirius Star*, a
tanker carrying 2 million barrels of crude oil worth
more than $100 million. It took the pirates only 20
minutes to chase down the ship, board the vessel,
and take command. To win the release of the tanker
and its crew, the Saudis were forced to pay a ransom.

Oil company executives and energy experts raised
alarms. They suggested that the pirates could do

anything from simply slowing oil deliveries to igniting the tankers, creating huge, floating infernos. Explained Donna J. Nincic, an associate professor of maritime policy at the California Maritime Academy of California State University:

> *An oil tanker of this size could cause significant environmental damage if run aground, sunk, or set on fire. . . . Had the pirates wished to run the ship aground, blow it up, or cause some other form of harm, it would have been relatively easy for them to do so.*[6]

The government of Somalia, which has been hobbled by years of civil war, is powerless to stop the pirates. Combat ships from the United States and other countries patrol the vicinity, but their efforts to stop the pirates have been mostly unsuccessful. The United States and its allies maintain a force of 20 ships patrolling the waters off East Africa,

Somalia's Strategic Position

Somalia is located just below the Gulf of Aden, which serves as an exit point for tankers that sail from Yanbu, a Saudi Arabian port city on the Red Sea. Ships sailing south through the Suez Canal also exit through the Gulf of Aden. Some 20,000 ships a year sail through the gulf, many of them tankers. Pirates using Somalia as a base have many opportunities to seize ships, take hostages, and demand ransom payments.

but officials said there is too much ocean to cover to stop the pirates. "It's 2.5 million square miles [6.5 million sq km] we're dealing with," said Lieutenant Matt Allen, a spokesperson for the US Navy's Fifth Fleet, which patrols the waters. "It's a very large area. It's a daunting task."[7]

In 2009, four armed pirates seized a US cargo ship, MV *Maersk Alabama*. Crew members were able to repel the pirates, but not before the pirates took hostages. After negotiating with the pirates, the *Maersk Alabama*'s captain, Richard Phillips, agreed to be taken captive in exchange for his captured crew members. Phillips was taken aboard a small boat, where he was held for nearly a week. The tense drama ended when Navy SEAL sharpshooters from the USS *Bainbridge* killed most of the pirates, freeing Phillips.

Although *Maersk Alabama* was not an oil tanker, world leaders hoped the US Navy's deadly action would convince the Somali pirates to stop preying on tankers as well as other shipping. But piracy continued anyway. In 2008 and 2009, there were more than 300 attacks on ships in the Indian Ocean committed by armed Somali gunmen. As long as Somalia is unstable, it will be difficult to stop the attacks.

*A French helicopter patrolled past suspected pirates
off the coast of Somalia in 2010.*

Car ownership is rapidly increasing in China and India, causing traffic jams including this one in Beijing in 2010.

DEMAND IN DEVELOPING NATIONS

According to the International Energy Agency, between 2005 and 2007 China and India were responsible for 70 percent of the increased energy demand in the world. The members of the new middle classes of India and

China were buying cars at a frenzied pace, increasing demand for oil in those countries. When demand rises, prices rise as well. With China and India becoming major energy consumers, the result has been higher prices for energy in the United States, Europe, and other parts of the world. It has meant that two countries that are on friendly terms with the United States pose a danger to US energy security—in this case, through higher prices at the gas pump. Americans feel the cost in other areas as well. Home heating oil prices rise, as do the prices of many products when their producers' energy costs go up.

"There's no end in sight of potential demand in China and India," said Maurice Lorenz, a former executive with the US oil company Exxon Mobil. "There's no stopping it. Somebody's going to have to meet the demand."[1]

Worldwide Car Sales

In 2007, worldwide car production topped 50 million vehicles for the first time and is likely to remain at that level, according to the International Organization of Motor Vehicle Manufacturers. Yearly international car production has been:

Year	Production
2008	52,940,559
2007	54,920,317
2006	49,886,549
2005	46,862,978
2004	44,554,268
2003	41,968,666
2002	41,358,394
2001	39,825,888
2000	41,215,653
1999	39,759,847

Source:
"Cars Produced in the World." *Worldometers*, worldometers. info. 2009. Web. 13 Sept. 2010.

TRAVELING TO SEE RELATIVES

China and India are the two most populated countries on the planet, each with populations of more than a billion people. For decades, neither country seemed to need to import energy. Until 1993, China was an oil exporter. To get around the crowded streets of their cities, most people did not rely on cars—they took public transportation or rode bicycles. For many years, rural parts of China and India did not have reliable electricity. Neither country needed more energy because their citizens used little power.

Things started to change in the 1990s as both countries moved toward industrialization. China and India have both developed economically, which means both countries now demand more energy. Moreover, the industrializations of China and India have created new middle classes in each country and, along with it, desires for more comfortable lifestyles. People are buying products—particularly automobiles. In China, car ownership jumped by 300 percent between 2002 and 2008. The Chinese add 1,000 cars to their city streets every day. The automobile market in India is considered just as robust—car sales grow by 15 percent a year.

As sport utility vehicles (SUVs) have become less popular in the United States because they get poor gas mileage, auto companies have had little trouble finding buyers for SUVs in China. For decades, many Chinese people found themselves stranded in their home cities, sometimes hundreds or thousands of miles away from relatives. Now that they have the money to travel and see their relatives, many Chinese people are buying SUVs to make these long-distance trips. "More and

What Does Gas Cost in China?

In 2008, gasoline prices topped four dollars per gallon (3.8 L) in the United States. Other industrialized countries saw prices rise as well. In China, though, motorists paid the equivalent of $2.50 per gallon (3.8 L). These artificially lower prices have helped many Chinese people afford cars. This has increased worldwide demand for oil—and helped drive up oil prices in the United States.

Why do the Chinese pay less for gas? As a Communist society, the Chinese government controls the nation's economy. In many other countries, supply and demand in the market dictate prices. In China, the government owns the country's three oil companies and sets the price of gas. When Chinese oil companies buy oil from international markets, they lose money when they sell the gasoline to consumers. The government is, therefore, keeping the price of gasoline artificially low. This loss has to be made up elsewhere, so other government-owned industries overcharge for goods. According to University of California, Los Angeles economist Donald H. Straszheim, the 2008 inflation rate in China—the rate of price increases for all goods—was 8 percent. In 2008, the inflation rate in the United States was less than 4 percent. Explained Straszheim, "The [Chinese] are paying for these low oil prices. They just don't see it at the pump."[2]

Compact cars such as this Volkswagen Polo, manufactured at the plant in Pune, are popular in India.

more people will choose jeeps, which are suitable for driving in the countryside," said Yan Yizhou, a 32-year-old Beijing sales manager who owns an SUV. "When your salary reaches a certain standard, you can buy a car and taste the fun of it."[3]

Meanwhile, in India, drivers tend to prefer compact cars, probably because the traffic seems forever snarled on busy city streets and drivers find it is easier to dart in and out of tie-ups in smaller vehicles. Small cars are also less expensive. That is why many major carmakers have established factories in India specifically to build tiny cars. Volkswagen, for example, opened a factory in 2009 in Pune, India, specifically to manufacture compact cars. Volkswagen hoped this compact car, the Polo, would help the company capture 10 percent of the Indian market. Ford, General Motors, and Nissan have also expanded into the country.

The governments of India and China believe they have every right to consume more energy and resources than they did in years past. They believe they have the right to industrialize and bring their people's standard of living up to the levels in the United States and Europe. They argue that long-term energy-guzzling countries such as the United States must curb their energy use, not China, India, and other developing countries.

Condemning Iran

With demand for cars so high in India and China, many experts fear that the growing need for oil in those two countries could eventually lead their leaders to establish closer relations with the United States' enemies—particularly Iran, which sits atop the world's third-largest supply of oil. Said Erica

S. Downs, a former CIA analyst who studies energy issues for the Brookings Institution, a think tank in Washington DC:

The challenge for America is to persuade Beijing to satisfy its oil demand in ways that do not support states whose behavior violates international norms. . . . Beijing's assessment of what constitutes bad behavior by other states and how it should be dealt with often differs from Washington's. [4]

Friendlier relations between China and Iran could have grave consequences for the United States. Iran has made no secret of its intentions to develop nuclear energy. While leaders of the country insist that they seek only to use nuclear energy to make electricity, US military leaders fear that the Iranians are secretly working to develop nuclear weapons. A nuclear-armed Iran could threaten Israel and other US allies in the Middle East.

Iran's Best Customers

Several US allies buy oil from Iran, making it unlikely they would agree to an embargo of Iranian oil. Japan, for example, has been a US ally since the end of World War II. However, the country buys more than 500,000 barrels of Iranian crude per day. In 2008, Iranian oil importers included:

Country	Thousand Barrels Per Day
Japan	520
China	430
India	410
South Korea	210
Italy	160
Spain	140
Greece	110
France	90
South Africa	90
Others	440
Total Exports	2,600

Source:
"Iran: Country Analysis Brief."
US Energy Information Administration. US Department of Energy, 2008. Web. 13 Sept. 2010.

China is a permanent member of the UN Security Council, which is the committee responsible for facilitating peace between nations. China could use its vote to help pressure Iran to give up its nuclear ambitions. One possible pressure could include embargoes on commerce with Iran. This would leave Iran few places to sell its oil and could bankrupt the country. However, China already buys a lot of oil from the Middle Eastern country and needs to continue purchasing Iran's oil to maintain its own growth. China has objected to sanctions against Iran in the past. If the Security Council ever voted to place an embargo on Iran, China might choose to veto it.

Late in 2009, the US government convinced the Chinese to sign a statement of disapproval toward the Iranians, demanding that they give up their nuclear ambitions.

China's Major Supplier

In addition to Iran, China relies on Sudan for oil. Sudan is another country that is hostile to US interests. According to the US Department of Energy, Sudan produces almost 500,000 barrels a day, much of which is sold to China. China also helps supply Sudan with weapons. The Sudanese government has been accused by international human rights groups of sponsoring genocide against nomadic Sudanese tribe members living in the Darfur region of the country. Estimates have placed the death toll as high as 400,000.

US diplomats believed the Chinese disapproval of Iran was an important first step. However, as China's energy demands continue to rise, they wonder if Chinese leaders will continue to disapprove of a country that keeps members of the new Chinese middle class on the road. In July 2010, the Chinese government backed away from its disapproval, saying that new European Union sanctions on Iran were too strict. The United States continued to push for Chinese cooperation.

Despite China's disapproval of Iran's nuclear development program, the two countries remain trading partners. Iran buys goods manufactured in China and China buys Iranian oil. "We mutually complement each other," explained Ali Akbar Salehi, Iran's former representative to the International Atomic Energy Agency. "They have industry and we have energy resources."[5]

The president of Iran, Mahmoud Ahmadinejad, defends his country's right to develop nuclear power.

Burning fossil fuels such as gasoline emits carbon dioxide.

FOSSIL FUELS
AND CLIMATE CHANGE

*O*il, coal, and natural gas are known as fossil fuels. Fossil fuels are made of compressed vegetation and animal remains that have been buried beneath Earth's surface for millions of years. Scientists agree that fossil fuels do not burn cleanly, but instead emit carbon dioxide. Carbon dioxide and other greenhouse gases trap the sun's energy in the atmosphere. Most scientists agree that the greenhouse gases emitted by human actions contribute to climate change.

Swedish physicist Svante Arrhenius first raised fears that Earth's climate was changing due to the burning of fossil fuels in 1896. He found that carbon dioxide and similar gases trap heat in the atmosphere and reflect it back to earth, creating a "greenhouse effect." In the late 1930s, Guy Stewart Callendar, a British engineer, asserted that the carbon dioxide content of the planet's atmosphere had increased by 10 percent since the 1890s. Soon, other scientists published studies supporting the theory that the planet's surface temperature was rising, and in 1979 the National Academy of Sciences

Warmest Decades on Record

The following statistics were released during the 2009 United Nations Climate Change Conference in Copenhagen, Denmark:
• A US National Academy of Sciences study of tree rings has found evidence that the past few decades were the warmest on Earth in the past 400 to 1,000 years.
• The University of Bern in Switzerland has concluded that carbon dioxide levels in the atmosphere are at their highest in the past 800,000 years.
• The National Aeronautics and Space Administration reported that since 1850, the five-warmest years on record were 1998, 2005, 2003, 2002, and 2004 in that order.

Glaciers such as this one in Argentina might shrink or disappear if climate change continues.

issued a report stating that global warming is a consequence of fossil fuel use. Over the years, the majority of scientific studies have concluded that the greenhouse effect is causing climate change.

Many experts believe global warming could lead to horrific consequences, including the melting of the polar ice caps, extinction and endangerment of species, and severe droughts and flooding. According to the Intergovernmental Panel on Climate Change (IPCC), if fossil fuel use continues on its current pace, the planet's temperature could rise by as much as 11.5 degrees Fahrenheit (6.4°C) by the end of the twenty-first century.

Even the lowest estimates, a change as low as 2 degrees Fahrenheit (1.1°C), could lead to rising sea levels and increased extreme weather. Coastal and island communities could be threatened. Storms and droughts both could be more severe. Agriculture and fishing could be disrupted, as well as any industries that rely on the current pattern of

Climate Refugees

Climate change is blamed for rising sea levels in the Pacific Ocean. Already, people who live on some Pacific islands have been forced to seek higher ground because high tides have swamped their homes. These people are known as climate refugees. "Communities all over the Pacific are alarmed at coastal erosion and the advancing sea levels," said Diane McFadzien, South Pacific regional climate coordinator for the World Wildlife Fund, an environmental group. "We are already seeing signs of whole villages having to relocate."[1] Potentially, 7 million people living on Pacific islands could become climate refugees, as well as others who live in low-lying coastal areas.

the seasons. An increase of 11.5 degrees Fahrenheit could easily be catastrophic to society and to the environment as humans know it.

RISING TEMPERATURES

There are already signs that Earth's ecology has changed due to global warming. In Canada, warmer winters have lengthened the lifespan of the pine bark beetle, which feeds on pine trees; large colonies of the beetles are believed responsible for killing millions of trees in British Columbia. And in

Is Clean Coal a Myth?

What if fossil fuels could burn without emitting carbon dioxide? Some scientists believe that carbon dioxide can be scrubbed from coal emissions. This concept is known as clean coal technology.

Also known as carbon capture and storage, the process catches carbon dioxide as the coal is burned, and then compresses it into liquid form. The liquid carbon dioxide is piped underground or into the ocean. In 2009, Congress appropriated $3 billion for grants to US power companies pursuing clean coal projects. Coal-fired plants produce about half the electricity used in the United States. If they can be made to burn cleanly, millions of tons of carbon dioxide would be kept out of the atmosphere.

Other scientists observe that carbon dioxide capture and storage does not get rid of the carbon dioxide; it simply puts it somewhere else. In addition, reducing emissions does not solve coal's problems. Coal mining harms the environment as forests are leveled and mountaintops are flattened. Mining is also dangerous for mine workers. Explained environmental writer Richard Conniff, "'Clean' is not a word that normally leaps to mind for a commodity some [people] . . . associate with unsafe mines, mountaintop removal, acid rain, black lung, lung cancer, asthma, mercury contamination, and, of course, global warming."[2]

Europe, warmer winters have
shortened the Alpine ski season.

According to the US Geological
Survey, polar bear populations have
been declining. Evidently, many
bears drown because the lengths they
have to swim from ice shelf to ice
shelf are getting longer, and many
of them grow tired and are unable to
make it to safety. Polar bears depend
on sea ice, where they hunt for seals
surfacing for air. If Arctic sea ice
shrinks, polar bears might starve as
they lose their hunting grounds. In
2008, the polar bear became the
first species protected under the US
Endangered Species Act because it
was threatened by climate change.

Said former US vice president Al
Gore, who shared the 2007 Nobel
Peace Prize with the IPCC for their
campaigns against global warming:

> The basic facts [about climate change]
> are incontrovertible. . . . The scientists

**Baseball
and Climate Change**

Even America's favorite
pastime, baseball, has
been affected by climate
change. Warmer winters
have extended the lifespan
of the emerald ash borer,
an Asian beetle that feeds
on ash trees. Ash is used
to make bats for the Major
League. Some 25 mil-
lion ash trees have been
killed by the beetle since
2002 throughout the Mid-
western and mid-Atlantic
states. Baseball bat manufacturers worry that they
will need to switch to a
different type of wood,
which could affect players'
performance.

have long held that the evidence in their considered word is "unequivocal," which has been endorsed by every national academy of science in every major country in the entire world.[3]

GOVERNMENT ACTIONS

In late 2009, representatives from 193 countries met in Copenhagen, Denmark, to work out a plan to lower carbon dioxide emissions. Most of the plan was negotiated by five of the world's largest carbon dioxide–emitting countries, including the United States, China, India, Brazil, and South Africa. The main feature of the plan required countries to establish carbon dioxide–emission goals. The agreement also committed the world's industrialized nations to provide $100 billion a year through the year 2020 to developing nations to help them create industries and jobs without relying on fossil fuels.

If the goals of the Copenhagen Accord are met, further global warming could be kept below a total increase of 3.6 degrees Fahrenheit (2°C). President Obama, who took a direct hand in negotiating the details of the agreement, said the Copenhagen Accord represents an important step toward limiting climate change, and he called on the nations of the world to reduce their reliance on fossil fuels. "We have come a long way, but we have much further to go," he said.[4]

Many environmentalists criticized the Copenhagen Accord, however, noting that the carbon dioxide–reduction commitments made by the industrialized countries are nonbinding. "It recognizes the need to keep warming below [3.6 degrees Fahrenheit], but does not commit to do so," said Jeremy Hobbs, head of Oxfam International, an antipoverty organization.[5]

In the difficult economic conditions of 2009 and 2010, experts believed it would be unlikely that the nations that signed the agreement would meet their targets. Nevertheless, the Copenhagen Accord represented the first substantial agreement among the world's biggest polluters, recognizing that it is time to cut emissions and

Climate Change Skeptics

Many people are not convinced that man-made pollution is responsible for global warming. They insist Earth has naturally gone through warming and cooling cycles, and that the current warming cycle should be no cause for alarm. US Senator James M. Inhofe of Oklahoma said, "Much of the debate over global warming is predicated on fear, rather than science. I [have] called the threat of catastrophic global warming the greatest hoax ever perpetrated on the American people."[6]

find sources of energy that do not endanger the fate of the entire planet.

In the United States, passing a comprehensive energy reform bill remained politically impossible in 2010. The nation remained divided on the issue, as some people disagreed on the scientific evidence and others believed it would be too expensive to change the country's energy use habits. Although the House of Representatives passed a climate change bill in 2009, the Senate failed to vote on its own version of the bill. Earlier, however, Congress passed other measures designed to cut down on carbon dioxide emissions. By 2020, all cars operating on US roads must be able to travel at least 35 miles per gallon (14.9 km/L), which is 7.5 miles more per gallon (3.2 km/L) than the standard in 2010.

Demonstrators protested against climate change outside the summit in Copenhagen, Denmark, on December 12, 2009.

New nuclear power plants are expensive, but some experts argue new plants improve a region's economy.

NUCLEAR POWER

In 2010, nuclear plants supplied 20 percent of electricity in the United States. Nuclear power is dependable, but new plants are costly to build. In 1996, the most recent commercial nuclear plant to go on line in the United States,

Unit 1 of the Watts Bar plant in Tennessee, cost
$7 billion and took 23 years to build. Eleven years
later, the plant's owner, the Tennessee Valley
Authority, gave approval for completion of Unit 2 at
Watts Bar at a cost of another $2.5 billion.

These huge costs are paid back by businesses and
homeowners in the form of high energy bills. A
study by the Washington DC think tank Center for
American Progress found that the cost of buying
electricity from new nuclear plants could be triple
what consumers pay now. "Estimates for new nuclear
power place these facilities among the costliest
private projects ever undertaken," argued the study.[1]
On the other hand, proponents argue that electricity
from existing nuclear plants is cheaper than
electricity from coal or natural gas power plants over
the long term.

Many experts argue for building new nuclear
plants. The administration of President Obama has
asserted that nuclear power is an important source
of energy supply in the United States. "I believe in
nuclear power as a central part of our energy mix,"
US Energy Secretary Steven Chu said in 2009.[2]

One reason political leaders support nuclear
plants is because they promote enormous economic

development. Corporations are more likely to open new factories or expand existing facilities when there is a guaranteed source of energy available nearby. According to a report by an economic development group, the Clean and Safe Energy Coalition, a nuclear plant can be expected to create $430 million per year in its local community. Therefore, nuclear reactors do more than make sure the lights go on at home—they are responsible for providing jobs.

By 2010, the US NRC had applications on file for 18 nuclear sites, although several

When Energy Provides Jobs

In 2008, a new nuclear power station was planned for Levy County, Florida. The local power company, Progress Energy, proposed a plant at a cost of $17 billion to be completed in 2017. In 2009, the county's unemployment rate climbed to approximately 12 percent.

Many residents of Levy County expressed no fears about the cost, environmental hazards, or safety of nuclear power. Instead, they looked forward to the steady paychecks employment at the plant would provide. "There's an awful lot of hope out here," said Bill Lake, mayor of the town of Inglis, which is where the plant will be located. [3]

Plans called for 3,000 local construction workers to build the plant and for another 800 people to work there after its completion. However, in 2009 and 2010, the plant hit several delays in financing, pushing the project back until at least 2020. It faced protests from people concerned about the environment and loss of wetlands and from people worried about radiation and what to do with spent nuclear fuel. Others argued that the money would be better spent investing in renewable energy. Some experts began to predict in the spring of 2010 that it was unlikely the plant would ever be completed.

were on hold. Said a report by Fitch Ratings, an international financial research company, "It is no longer a matter of debate whether there will be new nuclear plants in the industry's future. Now, the discussion has shifted to predictions of how many, where, and when."[4]

SAFETY AND ENVIRONMENTAL CONCERNS

Nuclear power has been a part of global society since the 1930s when scientists learned how to release enormous amounts of energy by splitting the atom in a process known as fission. In 1945, the United States brought World War II to a halt when US planes dropped atomic bombs on the Japanese cities of Hiroshima and Nagasaki, killing tens of thousands of people and obliterating both cities.

Soon after the war, engineers harnessed atomic power and began to use it to spin turbines, making electricity. In 1956, the first nuclear plant began

What Is Nuclear Fission?

Nuclear power plants depend on the energy that occurs during nuclear fission, the splitting of atoms to form smaller atoms. The uranium atom is easily split apart, so it is used during nuclear fission. When fission occurs, an enormous amount of energy is released. A nuclear plant changes some of that energy into heat to create steam, which drives turbines that make electricity.

During fission, a neutron strikes the uranium atom and splits it, releasing energy in the form of heat and radiation. When the atom is split, other neutrons are released, striking other uranium atoms. This causes a chain reaction, which continues releasing nuclear energy.

operations in Cumberland, England. In 1957, a nuclear plant near Pittsburgh, Pennsylvania, started delivering energy in the United States. In 2009, there were 104 nuclear reactors in 31 US states.

Nuclear power has safety risks, however. Nuclear fuel is radioactive and toxic. In 1979, a series of mishaps led to a near-catastrophe at the Three Mile Island nuclear plant near Harrisburg, Pennsylvania. The radioactive core of one reactor overheated and partially melted on March 28. The worst-case scenario, releasing radioactive material into the environment, did not occur.

Officials at the plant were eventually able to get the situation under control and cool the reactor core; nevertheless, thousands of people were evacuated from their homes in the region until the emergency passed. Today, Unit 2 remains shut down with no plans to restart it.

Seven years after the Three Mile Island accident, a much more serious incident occurred at a nuclear plant near the city of Chernobyl in Ukraine on April 26, 1986. It is believed that toxic gases were released into the atmosphere. Thousands of people might have been afflicted with radiation poisoning, which often causes cancer.

In the days following the partial meltdown, police guarded the entrance to the Three Mile Island nuclear plant.

Some scientists worry about what to do with spent nuclear fuel. It remains radioactive and, therefore, dangerous to people and the environment, for

Worldwide Uranium Reserves

Country	Tons	Approximate Percent of World Supply
Australia	1,673,000	31.0
Kazakhstan	651,000	12.0
Canada	485,000	9.0
Russia	480,000	9.0
South Africa	295,000	5.0
Namibia	284,000	5.0
Brazil	279,000	5.0
Niger	272,000	5.0
United States	207,000	4.0
China	171,000	3.0
Jordan	112,000	2.0
Uzbekistan	111,000	2.0
Ukraine	105,000	2.0
India	80,000	1.5
Mongolia	49,000	1.0
Others	150,000	3.0
World Total	5,404,000	

Source: "Supply of Uranium." *World Nuclear Association*. World Nuclear Association, Aug. 2010. Web. 13 Sept. 2010.

thousands of years. Spent nuclear fuel must be stored in secure containment facilities indefinitely. In 2006, the US EPA lengthened the time in which spent nuclear fuel must be stored from 10,000 years to 1 million years.

URANIUM RESERVES

Nuclear power relies on the mining of the element uranium. The World Nuclear Association, the international trade association for the nuclear industry, estimated in 2007 there were 5.4 million tons (4.9 million t) of uranium reserves available for mining. However, the world's 436 reactors consumed 65,000 tons (59,000 t) of uranium a year, meaning that worldwide uranium resources could run out in about 80 years. Some experts believe vast reserves of uranium have yet to be discovered. Between 2005 and 2007, the world's known uranium reserves increased by approximately 15 percent through new discoveries. Many believe this is a good indication that there is a lot more uranium left to be discovered, and they argue

Protection for 1 Million Years

The US EPA has ordered that all spent nuclear fuel be secured in containment facilities for at least 1 million years. Elizabeth Cotsworth, director of radiation for the EPA, said there is no way to tell whether the human race will still be around so far into the future; nevertheless, the agency must assume that 1 million years from now somebody will need to be protected from the hazards of radiation. "Most EPA rules apply for the foreseeable future—five or six generations," she said. "This rule is basically [for] 25,000 generations."[5]

nuclear power may be available for several hundred more years.

However, even if electric utilities in the United States were to make a bigger commitment toward nuclear power, it is likely that the nation would have to look elsewhere for its uranium. According to the World Nuclear Association in 2009, the United States contained only 4 percent of the world's known uranium reserves. Countries that held larger reserves included Kazakhstan, Canada, Australia, Namibia, Russia, Niger, and Uzbekistan.

A lack of uranium reserves means that, similar to oil, the United States will eventually have to rely on foreign governments to provide this energy source. Even so, many experts believe with the proper safeguards in place to protect people and the environment, nuclear power is a guaranteed source of energy that can be delivered to Americans for many years. Said Patrick Moore, chairman of the Clean and Safe Energy Coalition:

> *America . . . needs to look at all the available options for meeting increasing energy needs without sacrificing environmental principles. Nuclear energy won't be the only answer, but it is and always will be part of the solution.*[6]

Workers carefully transported spent nuclear fuel to a storage facility in Virginia.

Solar energy is one alternative to fossil fuels.

RENEWABLE ENERGY SOURCES

*A*s of 2008, Americans received only 7 percent of their electricity from renewable sources—hydroelectric, geothermal, wind, solar, and biomass. Some US leaders believe the country can do much better, eventually obtaining

100 percent of its electricity from renewable sources. Argued former vice president Al Gore:

> Scientists have confirmed that enough solar energy falls on the surface of the earth every 40 minutes to meet 100 percent of the entire world's energy needs for a full year. Tapping just a small portion of this solar energy could provide all of the electricity America uses. And enough wind power blows through the Midwest corridor every day to also meet 100 percent of US electricity demand.[1]

Other experts are skeptical, arguing that renewable sources will never be able to replace fossil fuels. One problem they cite is the huge investment necessary to build the infrastructure for solar, wind, geothermal, and other alternative facilities. Each type of renewable source has its own drawbacks and limitations, as well.

What Is Renewable Energy?

Energy is considered renewable when its source is not exhausted as it is used—in other words, it can easily be replaced. Although many renewable sources have been developed after years of scientific research, others have been used for thousands of years. The ancient Greeks built their homes so they would face the sun in the winter, taking advantage of the sun's natural warmth. Quaint windmills have dotted the landscape in Europe for centuries— inside, wind power turns millstones that grind grain. Anyone who has built a campfire has used biomass energy to cook food and provide warmth.

It has taken a considerable amount of science and engineering to make renewable sources available on a more widespread basis. In the 1950s, scientists at Bell Laboratories in New Jersey developed the first solar collectors

Has Oil Reached Its Peak?

Some renewable energy advocates urge industries and governments to develop solar, wind, and similar resources because they fear the supply of oil has already "peaked." They predict that oil will grow more difficult to draw out of the ground as some oil wells grow dry. Of course, as oil becomes harder to find and more expensive to pump, the prices of gasoline, heating oil, and other petroleum-based products will rise. "In the next few years, the supply [of oil] will tighten and this will lead to higher [oil] prices," insisted David Bowden, executive director of the Colorado-based Association for the Study of Peak Oil & Gas-USA (ASPO-USA).[2]

The numbers would seem to suggest that Earth's reserves can continue providing oil for decades to come—some estimates suggest crude oil reserves total about 1.25 trillion barrels. ASPO-USA argues that oil that has been cheap to find and pump will become scarcer and these supplies will begin running out as early as 2015. Afterward, geologists will have to find new oil fields and dig deeper to find sufficient supplies—which adds to the cost and the risk to the environment. Reported ASPO-USA, "Oil consumers ignore the peak oil problem at their peril."[3]

that were able to capture the energy of the sun and convert it into electricity. This is known as the photovoltaic process.

Solar energy is a promising technology, but it still has some unsolved challenges. Solar collectors only take in energy when the sun is shining, so solar-powered systems need ways to keep producing electricity at night and when the sky is cloudy. Scientists continue to improve batteries to store solar power for these times, but current batteries are expensive. Solar panels take up a lot of space and are also expensive to install. The technology will have to become cheaper to make it attractive to consumers.

WIND AND BIOMASS

Wind is another source of renewable energy. Tall windmill towers are located in areas that get a lot of wind. The wind turns blades located atop the windmills, spinning turbines to make electricity. Wind turbines are becoming less expensive, but building power lines from turbines in rural areas and windy coasts into cities still costs a lot of money. Wind power is only produced when the wind blows, making it impractical in some areas. Similar to solar power, storing wind power is expensive. In addition,

**No Profit
in Renewable Sources**

In 2009, Shell Oil, one of the world's largest energy companies, put its investments in solar and wind technology on hold. Shell had invested $1.25 billion in solar and wind power between 1999 and 2006, but concluded there would be no profit in these renewable energy sources. "We are businessmen and women," said Linda Cook, a spokeswoman for Shell. "If there were renewables [that make money] we would put money into [them]."[4] The company has made projections finding that by 2025, 80 percent of the world's energy will still be produced by fossil fuels.

biologists worry that wind turbines kill birds and bats, and homeowners often do not like having noisy turbines near their property.

Biomass, or organic matter, is also used to produce energy. Sources include wood, plants, manure, and trash. All of these materials can be burned in waste-to-energy plants to make electricity. Today, about 90 waste-to-energy plants in the United States burn trash and garbage to make steam, which spins turbines to make electricity.

Ethanol, made from corn, is used to supplement gasoline in cars. Most regular gasoline purchased from gas stations contains a small percentage of ethanol. Some cars are designed to run on ethanol blends containing 85 percent ethanol and 15 percent gasoline. Ethanol burns more cleanly and is less hazardous to people than gasoline. However, it is less fuel efficient, so cars have to burn more

A scientist examines blades of switchgrass, a plant that is being studied for use as an alternative fuel for cars.

of it. Current agriculture practices use a lot of fossil fuel for fertilizer and transportation to grow corn, so some experts argue ethanol does not truly replace

Biomass Provides Most Renewable Energy

As of 2007, biomass was the top source of renewable energy in the United States. Biomass provided 53 percent of the power generated by renewable sources. Much of the energy from biomass is created when wood or garbage is burned in waste-to-energy plants, which make steam that drives electric turbines. According to the US Department of Energy, other sources in 2008 were hydropower, 34 percent; wind, 7 percent; geothermal, 5 percent; and solar, 1 percent. In 2007, renewable sources made up 7 percent of the total energy needs of the United States.

gasoline. In addition, growing corn for fuel takes the place of other crops, which could lower the global food supply. Scientists are hopeful about the development of technology to allow other plants to take the place of corn. These plants, such as switchgrass, will grow in lands where food crops cannot grow and will not require fertilizer made from fossil fuels like corn does. Other scientists are experimenting with algae as a biofuel source. Algae biofuel has the highest yield per acre of any biofuel source.

GEOTHERMAL AND HYDRO

Geothermal power taps the heat of the Earth itself. To make geothermal energy, geologists look for trapped pockets of heat below ground. To bring the heat to the surface, engineers drill wells, then pump water into the wells, which reemerges as steam that is used to drive turbines.

Some of these trapped pockets are near the surface, but others are thousands of feet underground. In Lake County, California, north of San Francisco, geologists tap into a hotbed of geothermal energy, providing electricity for 800,000 homes. Unlike solar and wind power, geothermal power is available constantly. However, in some areas geothermal energy sources are found very deep underground and it is difficult and expensive to reach them. Other areas do not have enough geothermal activity to produce electricity with current technologies.

Another form of renewable energy is hydroelectric power—in simple terms, the use of moving water to create power. Hydroelectric power was first made in the United States in 1882 when engineers built a dam on the Fox River in Wisconsin. Today, the biggest source of hydroelectric power in the United States is the Grand Coulee Dam on the Columbia River in Washington State, which sends electricity to 11 states. Hydroelectric power is widely used in the United States, and it produces reliable, cheap, no-emissions energy. However, dams cause damage to the environment. When a river is dammed, a lake forms behind it, changing that area's habitat. This is a problem for fish, especially for salmon, which migrate upstream to lay eggs. In the Pacific Northwest region, several species of salmon are endangered because of dams. Dams also increase erosion, decreasing water quality. They cause large changes in the amount of water flowing down rivers, stranding fish and water plants when the water is low and flooding riverbanks when it is high. Engineers are working to create solutions to these environmental problems.

FORGING AHEAD WITH RENEWABLES

Despite the expense of developing renewable energy sources, many communities are forging ahead. The world's largest solar farm was scheduled to open in 2011 near Deming, New Mexico, where solar panels were planned over a 3,200-acre (1,300-ha) property. It was projected to supply enough power for 240,000 homes. In 2009, Public Service Electric & Gas Company, the largest electric utility in New Jersey, said it planned to spend $515 million to place solar modules atop some 900,000 utility poles in the state.

Adding renewable sources to substitute for coal and natural gas in power plants is well underway worldwide. It is more difficult to use alternate

sources to power cars and trucks,
which cannot stay plugged into the
electric grid the way a building can.
Automakers in the United States
and elsewhere are pursuing plans
to develop plug-in electric cars.
Some automakers already produce
hybrids, vehicles powered through a
combination of electric motors and
gasoline-fueled internal combustion
engines. As the name suggests, plug-
in cars would operate on electric
power only. The electric energy
would come from power plants.
Owners would be able to drive
50 to 100 miles (80.5 to 161 km)
on a single charge, then plug the car
into an ordinary house's electrical
system to recharge the battery. The
French automaker Renault hopes to
have plug-ins running on the streets
of Denmark, Australia, and Israel by
2011, where recharging and battery-
swap stations are being built, and in
the United States a short time later.

Energy Tax Credits

In 2008, Congress offered a tax credit to homeowners and businesses who began using renewable sources. Homeowners, for example, could receive tax credits worth 30 percent of the cost of installing solar systems, which typically cost as much as $40,000. Because of these tax incentives, the US Department of Energy projected that renewable sources could grow from providing 7 percent of US electricity in 2007 to 15 percent by 2030.

Many experts believe renewable sources could improve energy security. By obtaining energy from the sun, the wind, or Earth's own heat, Americans would rely less on oil imports. Said New Mexico Governor Bill Richardson, a former US energy secretary:

> *The country, even the world, can't stay on the energy path we have taken. It directly threatens our national interests and undermines our national security, and it is a path we have returned to again and again over the past thirty years despite embargoes, trade deficits, wars, and price shocks.*[5]

A man recharging an electric car in Guangzhou, China,
on August 4, 2010

President Richard Nixon signed an energy bill on May 7, 1974.

ENERGY INDEPENDENCE

I n 2007, Congress passed the Energy Independence and Security Act. The act required automakers to increase mileage standards for new cars, promoted the development of electric vehicles, devoted federal money toward developing solar energy, and increased energy efficiency in household appliances and lightbulbs.

Those steps were enacted to help the United States become more energy independent. Said the environmental group Natural Resources Defense Council:

> *This historic legislation will make America more energy independent, more secure, create thousands of new jobs, spark economic growth, save consumers money, cut pollution, and make real progress to reduce carbon [dioxide] emissions warming the Earth.* [1]

"THE MORAL EQUIVALENT OF WAR"

If the United States could truly obtain energy independence, its energy would be secure. No longer would the country have to rely on unstable foreign regimes to ensure a reliable energy supply. The notion of "energy independence" was first

---

Turning Off Incandescent Lights

As part of the 2007 Energy Independence and Security Act, incandescent lightbulbs will essentially be unavailable to buy by 2014. The act requires lightbulbs to use 25 percent less energy than the 2007 standard, an efficiency standard that manufacturers of incandescent bulbs would find difficult to meet. Incandescent bulbs glow when electricity passes through a tungsten filament, wasting energy as heat. The glass bulb becomes hot: that heat is wasted. Under new standards, homeowners will find themselves using compact fluorescent bulbs. The bulbs contain mercury vapor; the glow occurs as mercury atoms are excited by electricity, causing them to bounce around inside the bulb, striking a metal coating known as phosphors. Compact fluorescent bulbs are cooler, wasting less energy than incandescent bulbs.

advanced by President Richard M. Nixon in 1974 during the Arab oil embargo. He declared:

> *Let this be our national goal. . . . At the end of this decade, in the year 1980, the United States will not be dependent on any other country for the energy we need to provide our jobs, to heat our homes, and to keep our transportation moving.*[2]

Strategic Petroleum Reserve

Soon after the Arab oil embargo of 1973–1974, the federal government established the Strategic Petroleum Reserve, a stockpile of millions of barrels of crude oil that could be released into the US oil market if supplies were suddenly cut off. In 2010, the reserve held some 727 million barrels of oil, much of it stored in former salt mines along the coast of the Gulf of Mexico.

Only the president has the authority to approve releases from the reserve, which are sold to US oil companies at market prices. Although there have been loans made from the reserve to oil companies from time to time, there have been only two emergency draw-downs of the supply since it was established. In 1990 and 1991, on the eve of the Persian Gulf War, 17 million barrels were released from the reserve in anticipation that the conflict would reduce oil shipments through the Persian Gulf. Again, in 2005, 11 million barrels of crude were released from the reserve after Hurricane Katrina temporarily disabled several offshore drilling platforms in the Gulf of Mexico.

Other presidents have shared Nixon's enthusiasm for energy independence, but their efforts also have fallen short of success. Nixon's successor, Gerald R. Ford, signed the US Energy Policy and Conservation Act, which set fuel efficiency standards for cars for the first time. Ford predicted the

United States would achieve energy independence by 1985, five years later than Nixon had hoped.

In 1977, Ford's successor, Jimmy Carter, declared that energy independence should be a national priority, calling it the "moral equivalent of war."[3] Carter proposed a broad range of programs, including investment in renewable energy. He ordered solar panels installed on the roof of the White House and predicted that the United States would be energy independent by 1990.

Carter's successor, Ronald Reagan, had less interest in the issue of energy independence. He even had the solar panels taken off the White House roof. In 1991, Reagan's successor, George H. W. Bush, devoted $260 million in federal funds to help develop an electric car. In 1993, Bush's successor, Bill Clinton, added funds to the electric car program. And in 2001, Clinton's successor, George W. Bush, declared:

> *What people need to hear loud and clear is that we're running out of energy in America. We can do a better job in conservation, but we darn sure have to do a better job of finding more supply. . . . We can't conserve our way to energy independence.*[4]

Bush devoted $1.2 billion to the federal "Freedomcar" program, which sought to develop electric cars and alternative vehicles. He also put in solar panels on the White House grounds.

Barack Obama took office in 2009. His policies push for cleaner energy, more efficient energy use, and the prevention of climate change and environmental damage. Prior to the 2010 oil spill in the Gulf of Mexico, the administration was in favor of expanded offshore oil drilling. After the spill, new offshore drilling was put on hold for a time, but the ban was lifted on October 13, 2010.

ENERGY INTERDEPENDENCE

Many experts doubt that a national energy independence program could be successful. They argue the energy needs of the United States are too high for Americans to rely strictly on the energy produced at home. Daniel Yergin is an author and chairman of Cambridge Energy Research Associates, which helps governments form energy policies. He noted, "Energy independence . . . is increasingly at odds with reality."[5]

Instead, Yergin and other experts have argued for "energy interdependence," in which the United

*Offshore oil drilling allows the United States to produce more
of its own oil but exposes its coasts to environmental risks.*

States makes use of many more sources than it
does today. Under an expanded interdependence
program, if the energy were to be suddenly

interrupted from one source, such as the Persian Gulf, the disruption would have less effect on the US economy.

Economist Sebastian Mallaby shared worries about natural gas. He reported that 97 percent of US natural gas comes from US and Canadian sources. He explained:

> *If terrorists or a hurricane took out a key pipeline, it would be hard to bring in alternative supplies from outside North America, and prices would spike upward. By buying more liquefied natural gas from a diverse range of foreigners, the United States would reduce its energy independence but enhance its energy security.*[6]

ELUSIVE ANSWERS

Nevertheless, many experts believe energy independence is possible and, in fact, Americans have taken great strides to achieve independence since the 1973 oil embargo. For example, in 1973, 17 percent of the nation's electricity was produced in oil-fired plants; in 2008 only 1 percent of electricity in the United States was produced with oil. "Is energy independence a pipe dream? Hardly," insisted energy security expert Gal Luft:

In the electricity sector, the mission has already been accomplished. . . . Energy independence does not mean that the United States must be entirely self-sufficient. It simply means reducing the role of oil in world politics—turning it from a strategic commodity into merely another thing to sell.[7]

Some political leaders have argued for increasing oil exploration on US soil, suggesting that even protected areas and national parks be opened for production. Newt Gingrich, a former speaker of the US House of Representatives, advocated exploring for oil in the Arctic National Wildlife Refuge (ANWR), a 19-million acre (7.7-million ha) region in northern Alaska that is protected under federal law against industrial intrusions, including oil drilling. Gingrich argued that 10 billion gallons (37.8 billion L) of crude could be

Energy Independence and Bicycles

In 2008, New Mexico Governor Bill Richardson, a former US energy secretary, said one way to achieve energy independence was by riding more bicycles. Richardson said governments should encourage bicycle use by making more bicycling lanes available along city streets. He explained, "Places like London, Amsterdam, Copenhagen, and Paris have rainy, wet winters, like many of our cities. Yet people bike around and seem happy about it. There are dedicated bike lanes and trails so that riders don't have to worry about car conflicts and there are huge bike parking lots near train stations and commercial centers."[8]

pumped out of ANWR, a controversial figure that some experts argue is too high but others believe underestimates the oil that could be drilled. He said, "The United States may have dramatically more oil and natural gas reserves than we even know. But we will never find out if we can't or won't look."[9]

For Americans, energy security has remained an issue that is influenced by a number of factors. Hostilities in the Middle East and other unstable regions have often affected the price and availability of energy. A harsh winter can drive up home heating oil prices. Efforts by international lawmakers to reduce climate change could force industrialized nations to use less fossil fuel. Countries might have to spend billions of dollars to develop the infrastructure to deliver electricity made by the wind, sun, and other renewable resources to consumers. That is why political leaders, scientists, and engineers are likely to continue wrestling with the issue of energy security for many years to come, seeking answers that have so far eluded their predecessors.

US citizens and politicians argue whether oil drilling should be expanded in wilderness regions such as the Arctic National Wildlife Refuge.

TIMELINE

1896	1914	1930s
Swedish physicist Svante Arrhenius first suggests that fossil fuels emit gases that trap heat in Earth's atmosphere.	On the eve of World War I, Winston Churchill orders the British navy to convert from coal power to oil power.	British engineer Guy Stewart Callendar asserts that the carbon dioxide content of the Earth's atmosphere has increased due to fossil fuel use.

1977	1979	1979
On July 13, a massive power failure in New York City leads to a 25-hour blackout.	The National Academy of Sciences issues its first report stating that global warming is a consequence of burning fossil fuels.	On March 28, a series of mishaps leads to a partial core meltdown at the Three Mile Island nuclear power plant.

1957

The first nuclear plant in the United States begins making electricity.

1962

A trash fire in Centralia, Pennsylvania, spreads to a nearby coal mine, creating a mine fire that has never been extinguished.

1973

On October 6, Egypt and Syria launch attacks on Israel.

1979

In December, Islamic militants overthrow the regime of Iranian Shah Mohammad Reza Pahlavi.

1986

On April 26, an explosion at the Chernobyl nuclear power plant in Ukraine releases toxic gases into the atmosphere.

1989

On March 24, the oil tanker *Exxon Valdez* spills 11 million gallons (42 million L) of crude oil in Prince William Sound, Alaska.

TIMELINE

1990	2005	2005

On August 2, Iraq invades Kuwait, touching off the Persian Gulf War that ends in Iraq's defeat.

In August, hundreds of Ecuadoran protesters seize the country's oil fields.

President George W. Bush releases 11 million gallons (41 million L) from the Strategic Petroleum Reserve.

2008	2008	2008

On January 6, Iranian patrol boats harass US Navy warships in the Strait of Hormuz.

On November 17, Somali pirates hijack the *Sirius Star*, a Saudi Arabian tanker carrying 2 million barrels of crude oil.

On December 22, the walls of a coal ash pond near Kingston, Tennessee, burst open.

2006

In January, terrorists bomb natural gas and electrical lines leading to the Republic of Georgia capital, Tbilisi.

2006

The Environmental Protection Agency declares that all spent nuclear fuel must be contained for 1 million years.

2007

Congress adopts the Energy Independence and Security Act, requiring automakers to improve fuel efficiency.

2008

Congress provides homeowners and business owners with tax cuts to make use of wind, solar, and other renewable energy resources.

2009

On December 18, international leaders forge the Copenhagen Accord.

2010

On April 20, the Deepwater Horizon oil rig explodes, killing 11 workers and leaking 140 million gallons (530 million L) of oil.

ESSENTIAL FACTS

AT ISSUE

❖ The United States imports approximately 55 percent of its oil, often placing the United States at the mercy of hostile or unstable foreign regimes.

❖ The energy infrastructure of the United States can break down due to natural causes or mechanical problems.

❖ Carbon dioxide emissions from fossil fuels are most likely contributing to global warming.

❖ Developing nations such as China and India have put a strain on oil supplies, leading to higher prices.

❖ Renewable energy sources provide only 7 percent of the energy used in the United States.

❖ Terrorists may target pipelines, refineries, and other components of the world's energy infrastructure.

CRITICAL DATES

1973
Saudi Arabia and other Middle East oil states declared an embargo on oil shipped to the United States and its European allies, cutting off supplies for about six months.

December 1979
Islamic militants took control of the government of Iran. The new regime cut off oil supplies to the United States, leading to long-term hostilities between the two countries.

August 2, 1990
Iraqi dictator Saddam Hussein ordered an invasion of neighboring Kuwait, setting off the Persian Gulf War.

December 2009
Many of the world's nations met in Copenhagen, Denmark, to reach agreements about curbing carbon emissions to lessen climate change.

April 20, 2010

An oil rig, Deepwater Horizon, exploded in the Gulf of Mexico, killing 11 workers and causing an oil leak that gushed more than 140 million gallons (530 million L) of oil in the following months.

Quotes

"A reliable energy supply is one of the basic prerequisites for a functioning economy."—*Sascha Müller-Kraenner, energy analyst, Ecologic Institute*

"The country, even the world, can't stay on the energy path we have taken. It directly threatens our national interests and undermines our national security, and it is a path we have returned to again and again over the past thirty years despite embargoes, trade deficits, wars, and price shocks."—*New Mexico Governor Bill Richardson, former US energy secretary*

GLOSSARY

carbon dioxide

> A chemical compound emitted during the burning of fossil fuels. Carbon dioxide is a greenhouse gas, meaning it helps trap heat in the atmosphere, which contributes to climate change.

coal ash

> Also known as fly ash, the highly toxic remnant of coal after it is burned in electric generating stations and similar facilities. Coal ash contains mercury, arsenic, and lead.

crude

> The thick and syrupy natural state of unrefined oil as it comes from the ground.

embargo

> An act by a government to refuse to sell its goods to certain countries, or a decision by countries to refuse to buy goods from specific providers.

emission

> Something released into the air, such as carbon dioxide.

fossil fuels

> The category of fuels that are composed of animal and plant remains that have been compacted beneath the Earth since prehistoric times; fossil fuels include coal, oil, and natural gas.

greenhouse effect
> The situation that occurs when carbon dioxide and similar gases trap heat in the Earth's atmosphere, reflecting the heat back to the ground, just as a greenhouse traps the sun's heat to warm plants.

middle class
> A group of people in a society who fall economically between the wealthy and the poor. Members of the middle class usually have the economic means to afford homes, appliances, and automobiles.

photovoltaic
> Solar cells that convert sunlight into electricity.

renewable energy
> Energy generated from natural resources that are replenished. Renewable sources include solar, wind, geothermal, biomass, and hydroelectric power.

turbine
> An engine that turns by means of wind or water, causing a wheel or blades to spin.

uranium
> The radioactive element that is used to fuel nuclear power plants.

ADDITIONAL RESOURCES

SELECTED BIBLIOGRAPHY

Gingrich, Newt. *Drill Here, Drill Now, Pay Less*. Washington, DC: Regnery, 2008. Print.

Gore, Al. "Speech on Renewable Energy." *npr*. NPR, 17 July 2008. Web. 27 Aug. 2010.

Müller-Kraenner, Sascha. *Energy Security: Re-Measuring the World*. London: Earthscan, 2008. Print.

Richardson, Bill. *Leading by Example: How We Can Inspire an Energy and Security Revolution*. Hoboken, NJ: John Wiley & Sons, 2008. Print.

FURTHER READINGS

Bauder, Julia. *Is Iran a Threat to Global Security?* Farmington Hills, MI: Lucent Books, 2006. Print.

Hunnicutt, Susan. *Foreign Oil Dependence*. Farmington Hills, MI: Greenhaven Press, 2008. Print.

Povey, Karen. *Energy Alternatives.* Farmington Hills, MI: Lucent Books, 2009. Print.

Ruschmann, Paul. *Energy Policy.* New York: Chelsea House, 2009. Print.

Web Links

To learn more about energy security, visit ABDO Publishing Company online at **www.abdopublishing.com**. Web sites about energy security are featured on our Book Links page. These links are routinely monitored and updated to provide the most current information available.

For More Information

For more information on this subject, contact or visit the following organizations.

US Department of Energy (DOE)
1000 Independence Avenue SW, Washington, DC 20585
202-586-5000
www.energy.gov
The DOE provides many resources about energy-related issues for students. The department's Internet site includes links for how energy issues impact national security, how the use of energy affects the environment, and the new advances in science and technology that can help provide clean and renewable energy.

US Environmental Protection Agency (EPA)
Ariel Rios Building, 1200 Pennsylvania Avenue NW
Washington, DC 20460
202-272-0167
www.epa.gov
The EPA enforces regulations that protect the environment, including those that regulate the use of energy. The EPA monitors carbon emissions and helps develop emission standards for automobiles and trucks. Students can find many resources about greenhouse gases by visiting the agency's Web site.

SOURCE NOTES

Chapter 1. The Strait of Hormuz

1. Sheryl Gay Stolberg. "Bush Castigates Iran, Calling Naval Confrontation 'Provocative Act.'" *New York Times* 9 Jan. 2008: A-10. Print.

2. Ibid.

3. Ibid.

4. Michael T. Klare. *Resource Wars: The New Landscape of Global Conflict*. New York: Henry Holt and Co., 2001. Print. 73.

5. Edmund Blair. "Iran Building Naval Bases up to the Strait of Hormuz." *The Journal of Turkish Weekly*. Journal of Turkish Weekly, 30 Oct. 2008. Web. 11 Sept. 2010.

6. Walter Russell Mead. "Iran's Provocation." *Wall Street Journal* 10 Jan. 2008: A-14. Print.

Chapter 2. The Importance of Energy Security

1. Sascha Müller-Kraenner. *Energy Security: Re-Measuring the World*. London: Earthscan, 2008. Print. 21.

2. Richard Bessel. *Germany After the First World War*. New York: Oxford University Press, 2002. Print. 111.

3. "Chavez: Bush 'Devil,' US 'On the Way Down.'" *cnn.com*. Cable News Network, 20 Sept. 2006. Web. 11 Sept. 2010.

4. Tim Padgett. "Venezuela's Oil Giveaway." *Time*. Time Inc., 7 Feb. 2006. Web. 11 Sept. 2010.

5. "Background Note: Saudi Arabia." *US Department of State*. US Department of State, Apr. 2010. Web. 11 Sept. 2010.

6. "The Blackout: Night of Terror." *Time*. Time Inc., 25 July 1977. Web. 11 Sept. 2010.

7. Ibid.

Chapter 3. Rarely Safe, Cheap, and Reliable

1. Andrew Higgins. "Power and Peril: America's Supremacy and Its Limits." *Wall Street Journal* 4 Feb. 2004: A-1. Print.

2. David Frum. *How We Got Here: The 70's, the Decade That Brought You Modern Life*. New York: Basic Books, 2000. Print. 319.

3. Sascha Müller-Kraenner. *Energy Security: Re-Measuring the World*. London: Earthscan, 2008. Print. xi.

4. "Exxon Valdez Oil Found in Tidal Feeding Grounds of Ducks, Sea Otters." *Science Daily*. Science Daily, 16 May 2006. Web. 11 Sept. 2010.

5. Shaila Dewan. "Coal Ash Flood Revives Debate About Hazards." *New York Times* 25 Dec. 2008: A-1. Print.

6. Jeff Tietz. "The Great Centralia Coal Fire." *Harper's Magazine* February 2004: 47. Print.

Chapter 4. Terrorism and Piracy

1. "Energy Crisis As Georgia Freezes." *BBC*. BBC, 26 Jan. 2006. Web. 11 Sept. 2010.

2. C. J. Chivers. "Explosions in Southern Russia Sever Gas Lines to Georgia." *New York Times* 23 Jan. 2006: A-3. Print.

3. Gal Luft and Anne Korin. "Terror's Next Target." *The Journal of International Security Affairs*. JINSA, Dec. 2004. Web. 11 Sept. 2010.

4. Carla D'Nan Bass and Juan Forero. "Amid Tight Oil Markets, Protests Cut Back Output in Ecuador." *New York Times* 24 Aug. 2005: C-6. Print.

5. "Plant Security." *Nuclear Energy Institute*. Nuclear Energy Institute, 2009. Web. 11 Sept. 2010.

6. Donna J. Nincic. "Maritime Policy: Implications for Maritime Energy Security." *Journal of Energy Security*. Journal of Energy Security, 19 Feb. 2009. Web. 11 Sept. 2010.

7. Jeffrey Gettleman. "Pirates Seize Oil Tanker, US-Bound, Off Somalia." *New York Times* 1 Dec. 2009: A-6. Print.

Chapter 5. Demand in Developing Nations

1. Alex Tiegen. "Former Oil Executive Blames Market for High Gas Prices." *White River Junction (Vermont) Valley News* 15 June 2008: B-1. Print.

2. Donald H. Straszheim. "Why, in China, Gas is $2.49 a Gallon." *Forbes.com*. Forbes.com, 28 May 2008. Web. 11 Sept. 2010.

3. Maureen Fan. "Creating a Car Culture in China." *The Washington Post*. The Washington Post Company, 21 Jan. 2008. Web. 11 Sept. 2010.

4. Erica S. Downs. "How Oil Fuels Sino-US Fires." *Bloomsberg BusinessWeek*. Bloomberg, 4 Sept. 2006. Web. 11 Sept. 2010.

Source Notes Continued

5. Robin Wright. "Iran's New Alliance With China Could Cost US Leverage." *The Washington Post*. The Washington Post Company, 17 Nov. 2004. Web. 11 Sept. 2010.

Chapter 6. Fossil Fuels and Climate Change

1. Kristina Stefanova. "Climate Refugees in Pacific Flee Rising Sea." *The Washington Times*. The Washington Times, 19 April 2009. Web. 11 Sept. 2010.

2. Richard Conniff. "The Myth of Clean Coal." *Yale Environment 360*. Yale School of Forestry and Environmental Studies, 3 June 2008. Web. 11 Sept. 2010.

3. John Dickerson. "What in the Hell Do They Think Is Causing It?" *Slate*. Washington Post Newsweek Interactive, 8 Dec. 2009. Web. 11 Sept. 2010.

4. Arthur Max, Associated Press. "Obama Brokers Climate Accord." *Philadelphia Inquirer* 19 Dec. 2009: A-1. Print.

5. Ibid.

6. James M. Inhofe. "Climate Change Update, Floor Speech." *James M. Inhofe: US Senator—Oklahoma*. James M. Inhofe, 4 Jan. 2005. Web. 11 Sept. 2010.

Chapter 7. Nuclear Power

1. Joseph Romm. "The Staggering Cost of New Nuclear Power." *Center for American Progress*. Center for American Progress, 5 Jan. 2009. Web. 11 Sept. 2010.

2. Kent Garber. "Gauging the Prospects for Nuclear Power in the Obama Era." *US News and World Report*. US News and World Report, 27 March 2009. Web. 11 Sept. 2010.

3. Associated Press. "Fla. Town Warms Up to Proposed Nuclear Plant." *msnbc.com*. msnbc.com, 6 Oct. 2009. Web. 11 Sept. 2010.

4. Rick Lyman. "Town Sees Nuclear Plans as Boon, Not a Threat." *The New York Times*. The New York Times Company, 10 April 2006. Web. 11 Sept. 2010.

5. David Kestenbaum. "EPA Expected to Issue Million-Year-Long Regulation." *npr*. NPR, 24 Nov. 2006. Web. 11 Sept. 2010.

6. Patrick Moore. "Old Foes Welcome Clean Fuel." *Philadelphia Inquirer* 5 Nov. 2009: A-19. Print.

Chapter 8. Renewable Energy Sources

1. Al Gore. "Speech on Renewable Energy." *npr*. NPR, 17 July 2008. Web. 11 Sept. 2010.

2. David R. Francis. "$4 a Gallon Gas? Peak-Oil Experts Say Yes." *The Christian Science Monitor*. The Christian Science Monitor, 19 Oct. 2009. Web. 11 Sept. 2010.

3. "Peak Oil 202." *ASPO-USA: Association for the Study of Peak Oil & Gas-USA*. ASPO-USA: Association for the Study of Peak Oil and Gas, n.d. Web. 11 Sept. 2010.

4. Tim Webb. "Shell Dumps Wind, Solar and Hydro Power in Favor of Biofuels." *guardian.co.uk*. Guardian News and Media Unlimited, 17 March 2009. Web. 11 Sept. 2010.

5. Bill Richardson. *Leading by Example: How We Can Inspire an Energy and Security Revolution*. Hoboken, NJ: John Wiley & Sons, 2008. Print. 11.

Chapter 9. Energy Independence

1. House Speaker Nancy Pelosi. "What Others Are Saying About the Historic Energy Bill." *Speaker Nancy Pelosi*. Nancy Pelosi, 18 Dec. 2007. Web. 13 Sept. 2010.

2. Ronald Bailey. "Energy Independence: The Ever-Receding Mirage." *Reason.com*. Reason Magazine, 21 July 2004. Web. 13 Sept. 2010.

3. Ibid.

4. Ibid.

5. Daniel Yergin. "Ensuring Energy Security." *Foreign Affairs* March–April 2006: 69. Print.

6. Sebastian Mallaby. "What 'Energy Security' Really Means." *Washington Post* 3 July 2006: A-21. Print.

7. Gal Luft. "Iran and Brazil Can Do It. So Can We." *The Washington Post*. The Washington Post Company, 6 July 2008. Web. 13 Sept. 2010.

8. Bill Richardson. *Leading By Example: How We Can Inspire An Energy and Security Revolution*. Hoboken, NJ: John Wiley & Sons, 2008. Print. 96–97.

9. Newt Gingrich. *Drill Here, Drill Now, Pay Less*. Washington, DC: Regnery, 2008. Print. 46.

INDEX

ABOUT THE AUTHOR

Hal Marcovitz is the author of more than 150 books for young readers. A former newspaper reporter, Marcovitz lives in Chalfont, Pennsylvania, with his wife Gail and daughter Ashley. In 2009, the Marcovitz family converted their home to solar power.

PHOTO CREDITS

iStockphoto, cover, 3, 56, 64, 74, 91, 97; Bill Foley/AP Images, 6; Map Resources/Red Line Editorial, Inc., 11; U.S. Navy/AP Images, 13, 98 (bottom); Thor Swift/AP Images, 15; Jeremy Edwards/ iStockphoto, 16; Leslie Mazoch/AP Images, 19; Ariana Cubillos/AP Images, 21; AP Images, 25, 26, 48, 79, 86, 96 (left); John Gaps III/AP Images, 30, 98 (top); Eric Gay/AP Images, 35; Don Wilkie/ iStockphoto, 36; EU NAVFOR/AP Images, 43; Imaginechina/ AP Images, 44, 85; Richard Drew/AP Images, 53; David Parsons/ iStockphoto, 54, 99; Peter Dejong/AP Images, 63; Paul Vathis/ AP Images, 69, 96 (right); Red Line Editorial, Inc., 70; The Daily Progress, Bill Clark/AP Images, 73; Al Grillo/AP Images, 95

A LITTLE

VIETNAMESE
C O O K B O O K

TERRY TAN

Illustrated by SHERRY TAY

CHRONICLE BOOKS

SAN FRANCISCO

First published in 1995 by
The Appletree Press Ltd
19–21 Alfred Street, Belfast BT2 8DL
Tel. +44 232 243074 Fax +44 232 246756
Copyright © 1995 The Appletree Press, Ltd.
Printed in the E.U. All rights reserved.
No part of this publication may be reproduced or
transmitted in any form or by any means, electronic or
mechanical, photocopying, recording or any information
and retrieval system, without permission in writing from
Chronicle Books.

A Little Vietnamese Cookbook

First published in the United States in 1995 by
Chronicle Books, 275 Fifth Street,
San Francisco, California, 94103

ISBN 0-86281-8118-1

9 8 7 6 5 4 3 2 1

Introduction

Of all the cuisines in the Indo-Chinese region, Vietnamese is probably the most strongly indigenous despite centuries of influence from the Asian sub-continent and, more recently, France. There are still echoes of Gallic elements and ambience in the baguettes and pâtés found in the coffee shops and the restaurants in the major cities. Vietnamese culture derives from a rich mélange of Melanesian, Indonesian, Negrito, and ancient Thai dating back some four thousand years. One thousand years of Chinese domination, and burgeoning trade between China and India, touched Vietnamese culinary evolution lightly. The cuisine remains at once delicate, complex, and sophisticated, drawing much from Chinese techniques, indigenous ingredients, Indian spices, and French finesse. Noodles, or *pho*, are ubiquitous throughout the land and the keynote flavor comes from *nuoc mam*, a fish sauce more pungent than other Southeast Asian fish sauces. What characterizes the cuisine are the fundamental seasonings of chilies, pepper, garlic, sugar, lime, coriander, and vinegar. There are, naturally, many similarities between Vietnamese dishes and those of Thailand, Burma, Laos, and Kampuchea, all of which share the same Indo-Chinese cultural heritage. Just as you would with those cuisines, use your instincts and personal taste when measuring such sharp flavors as chili, lime, pepper, and ginger – the top notes in Vietnamese cuisine.

A note on measures
Spoon measurements are level except where otherwise indicated. Seasonings can of course be adjusted according to taste. Recipes are for four people.

3

The Vietnamese Kitchen

First, very little special equipment is needed for Vietnamese cooking. A heavy and sharp cleaver, small paring knives, a good chopping board, and a heavy pestle or mortar are the fundamentals. A coffee grinder will do in place of the latter. Second, as the cuisine comes closest to Chinese, you can obtain most of what you need from a typical Chinese supermarket.

Dried Shrimp Paste (mam tom). Alternatives are Malaysian *belachan* or Thai *kapi*, similar products. Anchovy sauce comes quite close.

Dried Mushrooms (nam dong co). Chinese mushroom caps with a husky flavor. Must be soaked until soft before adding to stews and soups.

Fermented Bean Curd (chao-do). A red or white strong-flavored bean curd cheese, not to be confused with the fresh variety called *tofu*.

Fish Sauce (nouc mam and nouc cham). The first is a thin but pungent sauce made from salted anchovies and other small fish. *Nouc cham* is a blend of fish sauce, garlic, chilies, sugar, and lime, and integral to the Vietnamese meal. Both can be used as seasonings or dips.

Five Spice Powder (ngu vi huoung). Aromatic Chinese seasoning consisting of powdered star anise, cloves, cinnamon, fennel, and Sichuan pepper.

Golden Needles (dried lily buds). Used in Chinese cooking, the hard tips have to be cut off before using.

4

Lemon Grass (xa). Grass-like roots. Use only two inches of the root end, ground into paste.

Mint (bac ha). Often interchangeable with sweet basil as a garnish for soups.

Palm Sugar (duong the). Also known as jaggery. It is used in place of processed white sugar.

Plum Sauce (cuong ngot). Thick bottled sauce sometimes spiced with chilies used in sweet-and-sour dishes and as a dip base.

Rice Alcohol or spirit (ruou de). Fermented from steamed rice. Difficult to obtain, but any Chinese wine or sherry make good substitutes.

Rice Noodles (banh pho). Thick, wide, flat noodles that are sold dry or fresh.

Rice Paper (banh tranhg). Thin, dry wrappers used for Vietnamese spring rolls. Very delicate and brittle to handle, they must be soaked in water to soften.

Rice Vermicelli (bun). Transparent noodles, sold commercially as cellophane noodles and treated like any other dry noodle.

Star Anise (hoi). The dried fruit of a Chinese tree in a small star shape.

Salted Black Beans (tuoung hot den). Salty and slightly spiced dried soy beans for stir-fried dishes.

Pho

Basic Beef Soup

This is the most typical of Vietnamese soups and one that appears on every restaurant menu. It takes a few hours to make but the result is ambrosial. A crisp salad of bean sprouts, fresh coriander, and local vegetables is served on the side with a dip of *nuoc cham* (see p. 35).

---

4 lb beef rib bones	**Salad**
³/₄ lb stewing steak	¹/₂ lb fresh bean sprouts
10 cups water	1 sprig fresh coriander
1 large onion, sliced	1 stalk spring onion
thumb-sized piece of fresh ginger root, bruised	**Dip**
	1 tsp chopped red or green chilies
2 star anise	2 tbsp nuoc mam
¹/₂ tsp black peppercorns	half a lime or lemon
nouc mam *to taste*	
³/₄ lb beef fillet	

Put beef bones and stewing steak in a large saucepan with water. Add sliced onions, bruised ginger, anise, and peppercorns and bring to a boil. Turn heat low and simmer, covered, for 2–3 hours. Add *nuoc mam* to taste. You should be left with roughly 4 cups of rich stock. Strain stock, remove bones and stewing steak. Slice beef fillet very thinly. Blanch a few slices of beef for each portion, ladle soup into each bowl, and place beef on top. Traditionally, Vietnamese beef soup contains rice noodles but you can use any kind of noodles, either fresh or dried, blanched, and added to the bowl. Mix together salad ingredients. Mix together dip ingredients. Serve with chopped coriander on the side.

Canh Bun Tau

Fish and Cellophane Noodle Soup

Cellophane noodles are common to all Southeast Asian cuisines and are sold dried. The only noodles made from mung bean flour, they are used frequently in Vietnamese cold side dishes. Before cooking, soften for a few minutes in warm water. Remarkably, they keep their texture even with long cooking.

½ lb white fish (halibut or cod are excellent)	½ tsp turmeric powder
1 tsp ground ginger or purée fresh ginger	4 sweet basil leaves
½ tsp salt	1 tsp dried shrimp paste or anchovy sauce
1 tsp black pepper	5 cups water
2 tbsp vegetable oil and 1 tbsp peanut or sesame oil	juice of 1 lemon
2 cloves garlic, chopped	2 tbsp nuoc mam
½ large onion, sliced	1½ oz cellophane noodles, soaked until soft
	2 stalks spring onions, chopped

Chop fish coarsely and cover with ginger, salt, and pepper. Set aside. Heat oils in large saucepan and fry garlic and onions until light brown then add turmeric, basil, and shrimp paste. Add water, lemon juice, *nuoc mam* and bring to a boil. Add fish and cook for 4 minutes. Add noodles and serve in individual bowls with chopped spring onions.

Canh Chua Ca

Sweet and Sour Fish Soup

This is a south Vietnamese recipe that is often served alone as the evening meal. It is a hearty soup that can be made with many ingredients such as fish or meat and served with raw vegetable garnishes.

---

3 tbsp tamarind paste or 3 tbsp lime juice
7 cups water or fish stock
2 tbsp palm or white sugar
2 large tomatoes, skinned and sliced
1 thick stalk celery, chopped
1 tbsp nouc mam
10 oz cod or white fish fillets, cut into bite-size pieces
3 oz bean sprouts
1 tsp finely chopped red chilies
mint, sweet basil or fresh coriander leaves

Steep tamarind paste in cold water from allowance and strain into pot or, if using lime juice, add it to the water or fish stock. Combine liquid, sugar, tomatoes, celery, and fish sauce, and simmer for 15 minutes. Add fish, bean sprouts, and chilies and simmer for 3 minutes. Serve in individual soup bowls and garnish with plenty of mint, sweet basil or coriander, or all three. Serve with a side dip of *nouc cham* (see p. 35).

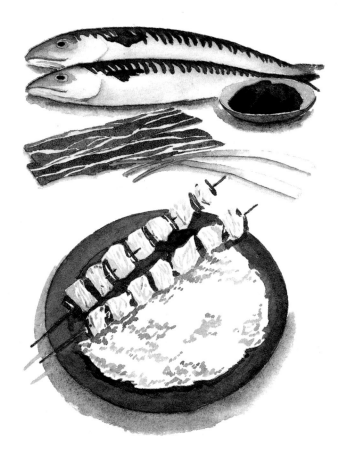

Cha Ca Nuong

Fish Brochettes

A north Vietnamese dish that celebrates what was once a famous road in Hanoi called "Pho Hang Cha Ca", now called by another name. These delicious fish brochettes are much revered as a festive dish, and are wonderful for barbecues. The use of bacon is part of Vietnam's French heritage. Any firm-fleshed fish can be used.

---

1 lb fish (cod, halibut or even mackerel)
2 strips streaky bacon (de-rinded)
2 tbsp vegetable oil
2 stalks spring onions, chopped
2 tbsp chopped peanuts
Marinade:
3 tbsp vegetable oil
2 tbsp nouc mam
2 tbsp rice spirit, Chinese wine, or sherry
1 tsp turmeric powder
1 tbsp grated ginger
2 tsp shrimp paste

Gut and clean fish and cut into bite-size chunks. Mix marinade ingredients together in a bowl and steep fish for several hours, turning over once or twice. Cut bacon into 1 inch squares. Thread alternate pieces of fish and bacon on metal or bamboo skewers. Heat 2 tablespoons of vegetable oil gently and add chopped spring onions. Blend with the marinade and baste the brochettes with this mixture as you barbecue or broil. When done, the fish should be opaque and the bacon sizzling. Serve, sprinkled with peanuts, over a bed of rice.

Cha Gio

Crispy Spring Rolls

Quintessentially Vietnamese, these delicate, crispy rolls are a refinement from the more robust Chinese rolls. The basic ingredient is minced pork, to which either prawns or crab can be added for savory flavor. The gossamer thin *bang tranhg* (rice paper) is hard to handle. You can use conventional spring roll skins as an easy alternative, but you won't achieve the same crispy results.

2 oz translucent rice vermicelli or cellophane noodles, chopped	4 oz water chestnuts, chopped
2 tbsp dried tree ears (wood fungus or wood ears), soaked until soft and chopped	2 stalks spring onions, chopped
	2 tbsp nuoc mam
	1 tsp pepper
	1 egg, lightly beaten
3 Chinese mushroom caps, soaked until soft and chopped	12–14 sheets banh tranhg
	vegetable oil for deep frying
6 oz minced pork	cornstarch (optional)

Put all ingredients except skins or rice paper in a large mixing bowl and blend well. Adding a tablespoon of cornstarch will give the mixture a smooth texture, but this is optional. To adjust seasoning, boil a small nugget of mixture and taste. Adjust seasoning if necessary. In a bowl of tepid water gently lower each sheet of *bang tranhg* or spring roll skin until soft and shake off excess water. Very carefully, lay sheets on a clean chopping board. Place a heaped tablespoon of mixture on sheet or skin, roll over once, and fold in sides. Roll over once more and tuck in firmly, patting the ends down. Finish making rolls as oil heats in the wok. Gently lower each roll in the oil to deep fry – a few at a time until light brown and crisp. Serve with fresh lettuce and mint leaves with *nuoc cham* (see p. 35).

16

Muc Don Thit

Stuffed Squid

Squid has an undeserved bad press due to over-cooking but is much loved all over Southeast Asia. Properly cooked squid, either stuffed or cooked quickly, will lay to rest any memories of rubbery tubes. The best size squid to use are those no larger than 2-inch body length. The filling for crispy spring rolls can do double duty here if you are making both dishes at the same time as the mixture is similar.

---

12 squid, cleaned and heads removed
1 oz transparent vermicelli, soaked until soft and chopped
4 Chinese mushrooms, soaked until soft and chopped
10 dried golden needles (lily buds), soaked until soft and chopped
5 oz minced pork
1 clove garlic, minced
1 stalk spring onion, chopped
1 tbsp nuoc mam
1/2 tsp pepper
1 egg, lightly beaten
6 tbsp oil

Dip hands in salt and rub grey membrane off squid. Remove the central quill-like bone and wash each squid thoroughly. Pat dry. Combine all ingredients except oil and adjust seasoning after tasting a boiled nugget of mixture. Fill each squid with mixture, but not tightly, as squid will shrink a little when cooked. Close each neck with toothpicks. Arrange in a steamer and cook for 10 minutes. Allow to cool completely. Heat oil and shallow fry squid until light brown. Serve hot or cold, and sliced into rings.

Thit Chua Xao Mang Tay Hop

Crab with Asparagus

Canned asparagus simply will not do for this dish – seek out fresh asparagus or imported asparagus stalks from Thailand that are thinner and have more crunch. Recipes with asparagus speak of the French influence in Vietnamese cuisine, just as the predominance of stir-frying in northern Vietnamese dishes reflects Chinese elements.

14 asparagus stalks, trimmed	1 tbsp cornstarch dissolved in
1 seafood or vegetable stock cube	a little water
4 fl oz water	8 oz crab meat
pinch of black pepper	1 egg white, lightly beaten
1 tbsp nouc mam	1 tbsp sesame oil

Trim off about ¹/₂ inch of the thick ends of asparagus as they can be pithy. Cut each stalk into 1¹/₂ inch lengths. Bring a large pot of water to a boil and blanch asparagus for 3 minutes. Remove and keep warm. Dissolve stock cube in 4 fluid oz water and bring to a boil. Add seasoning, *nouc mam*, and cornstarch liquid and simmer until thick. Add crab meat and lower heat. Stir in egg white and sesame oil and remove from heat. Pour over asparagus and serve immediately. Asparagus can also be cooked whole and served with this sauce.

Ga Xao Xa Ot

Chicken with Lemon Grass

It's not surprising that this dish echoes Thai, Laotian, and Indonesian elements as lemon grass is fundamental to all these cuisines. The traditional Vietnamese way to cook this dish is to cut up a large chicken on the bone, but chicken breasts will do nicely. Some chefs cook a braised version, but this stir-fried variation reflects Vietnam's Chinese culinary heritage in method if not ingredients as curry powder, lemon grass, and chilies are not used in Chinese cuisine.

1 1/2 lb chicken breast, sliced thickly	2 stalks spring onions
1 tsp pepper	1 tsp curry powder
1 1/2 inch lemon grass root, finely chopped	1 tsp salt
	2 cloves garlic
1 fresh red chili, sliced	2 tsp palm or white sugar
2 tbsp oil	1 tbsp nuoc mam
	2 tbsp chopped peanuts

Mix chicken slices with pepper, lemon grass, and sliced chili and set aside. Heat oil and fry chicken slices for a few minutes until chicken turns opaque. Remove and set aside. Pound spring onions with curry powder, salt, garlic, and sugar. Cover chicken to this mixture and set aside for an hour. Heat a little oil and fry chicken over high heat for 4 minutes. Add *nuoc mam* and sprinkle a little water over to moisten. Remove to serving plate and add chopped nuts. Garnish with chopped fresh coriander and serve with boiled rice or noodles. Leave out chili if curry powder is fiery.

Chim Cut Ro-Ti

Hot and Spicy Quail

Vietnamese are fond of game birds, especially in the north where there is not as great a variety of food as in the south. The use of chili peppers is the legacy of Portuguese visitors who arrived as early as the sixteenth century. As quail are small, allow one whole bird per person.

---

4 dressed quail	1 tsp chili powder or paprika
4 tbsp sesame oil	1 tbsp nouc mam
Marinade:	1 tbsp palm sugar
2 tbsp vegetable oil	1 tsp salt
3 cloves garlic, crushed or	2 tbsp water
1 tbsp garlic purée	lime juice
4 spring onions, chopped	
1 1/2 in of lemon grass root, chopped	

Split quail down the bony side and flatten to get a broad breast. Score breast with deep cuts. Make the marinade by heating vegetable oil in a skillet and frying garlic, onions, and lemon grass for a few minutes. Add chili powder, *nouc mam*, sugar, salt, and water and simmer for 3 minutes. Remove and cool. Marinade quail and chill for two hours. Heat broiler or barbecue and broil for 15 minutes on each side, basting frequently with sesame oil and marinade, until bird is crisp, aromatic and sizzling. Serve with a good squeeze of lime juice over quail.

Note: If you don't have a broiler, roast quail in a hot oven for 30 minutes, turning once and basting frequently.

Ga Nuoung Ngu Vi Thiong

Grilled Chicken with Five Spices

The use of five spices in Vietnamese dishes puts them firmly within the Chinese culinary sphere. However, there is an inevitable fine tuning to this recipe that makes it radically different from an uncompromisingly Chinese dish. Five-spice powder is quite strong, so use it judiciously. Pork pieces can also be used for this favorite barbecue dish.

---

2 spring chickens, about 3 lb each
Marinade:
4 tbsp vegetable oil
1 tbsp Crisco
10 shallots, finely sliced
4 cloves garlic, crushed
1 cup rice spirit or sherry
4 tbsp light soy sauce
2 tsp five-spice powder

Bone chicken and cut into large chunks. Make the marinade by heating the oil and Crisco and frying the shallots and garlic until light brown. Add rice spirit, soy sauce, and five-spice powder and pour immediately over chicken, rubbing it well in. Set aside for half an hour. Drain chicken and thread on skewers. Broil over charcoal, or whatever barbecue facilities you have, for 15 minutes on each side basting frequently with marinade until chicken pieces are slightly charred. Serve with a chili sauce or *nuoc cham* (see p. 35) and bread or rice.

Thit Bo Xao Mang

Stir-fried Beef with Bamboo Shoot

The French influence in Vietnamese cooking is still strong and most beef is cooked medium rare – even in the classic *pho* noodle dishes. This dish is an amalgam of Chinese, French, and Vietnamese cooking. For best results use a good cut of beef.

---

8 tbsp vegetable oil
2 tbsp sesame oil
12 oz sirloin or fillet beef, sliced thinly
2 stalks spring onions, cut into 3/4-inch lengths
2 cloves garlic, crushed
4 oz bamboo shoots, sliced
2 tbsp nouc mam
1 beef stock cube (optional)
1 tbsp sugar
2 tbsp cornstarch, dissolved in little water

Heat vegetable and sesame oil in a skillet until smoking and quickly fry beef slices for 1 minute. Drain thoroughly and set aside. Remove half of the oil, add spring onions and garlic. Fry for 2 minutes. Add all other ingredients and fry for a few minutes until thick and glistening. Add beef and toss rapidly until well covered and sauce is just thick enough to coat but not drown the beef. Serve garnished with chopped fresh coriander.

Thit Ga Nuong Chao

Grilled Chicken with Fermented Bean Curd

Though Vietnamese palates are attuned to spices, they also like the rich, savory unspiced dishes that come from the classical Chinese kitchen. Fermented bean curd is a fundamental Chinese ingredient usually cooked with chicken, eels, and tofu and has a redolence not found in any other ingredient. It is worth keeping a jar of it in your refrigerator as it keeps indefinitely. Fermented bean curd is either white or red, the latter having a rich, red gloss.

---

1 medium chicken, about 4 1/2 lb in weight
1 tsp black pepper
4 tbsp vegetable oil
Marinade:
2 squares fermented bean curd, and a tbsp of its juices
10 shallots, sliced
6 cloves garlic, crushed
2 tbsp palm sugar
2 tbsp rice spirit or sherry
pinch of ground cloves
1 cinnamon stick, about 2 inch

Chop chicken into bite-size pieces. De-bone if you prefer, but cooking chicken on the bone yields a richer flavor. Mix together the marinade ingredients and marinate chicken for several hours turning once or twice. Dust chicken with black pepper. Heat oil and fry chicken gently, sweating out all the juices to let it cook in its own richness until almost dry. Remove and finish cooking under a hot grill or on a barbecue (about 10 minutes). Serve with cucumber slices and rice.

Trung Hap

Steamed Egg with Mushrooms

This dish is from south Vietnam where cooking is relatively simple and the ingredients are allowed to speak for themselves. It's a light and complimentary dish to richer dishes on a typical dinner menu. The region is hot and humid and a heavy dish can be unpleasant after a hard day's work on the farms.

---

4 dried Chinese mushroom caps, soaked until soft and sliced
4 oz minced pork
4 oz prawn meat, chopped
4 eggs, lightly beaten
2 spring onions, chopped
2 tbsp fresh coriander, finely chopped
1 tbsp nuoc mam
1 tsp ground black pepper

Discard stems from mushrooms and squeeze out moisture. In a bowl, mix pork, mushrooms, prawns, and beaten egg. Add spring onions, coriander, fish sauce, and pepper. Mix well. Transfer to a deep bowl and pat down firmly. Place bowl in a wok and fill the wok with boiling water up to two-thirds of bowl. Cover wok, put on heat, and steam for 10 minutes, then uncover wok and cover bowl with a plate to prevent too much condensation collecting on top. Steam for another 20 minutes. Remove bowl from wok and turn out on a plate. Serve garnished with a sprig of fresh coriander.

Nuoc Cham

Chili, Garlic, and Fish Sauce

Piquant dips do double duty as condiments and seasonings in Vietnamese cooking. The base for these is always *nuoc mam* and you can add ingredients such as lime juice, chopped chilies, chopped nuts, spring onions, fried garlic, ginger and fresh herbs such as coriander, sweet basil, and mint.

---

4 red chilies
2 cloves garlic
1 tsp sugar
2 limes, peeled and chopped
1 tbsp hot water
1 tbsp vinegar
5 tbsp nuoc mam

Remove stalks from chilies and de-seed if you want a milder dip, though this defeats the purpose of *nuoc cham*. Pound garlic in a pestle and add chilies one by one, processing until you get a fine paste. Add sugar and lime pieces and pound to a pulp. Remove to a small sauce bowl and add water, vinegar, and fish sauce. Mix well and serve. Variations on the sauce can include chopped coriander, chopped ginger, pineapple, and any fresh herbs.

Tom Bam

Shrimp Paste

This is a pungent sauce and an acquired taste. It is usually added to soups but it can also serve as a dip for those with a fondness for fishy sauces. The traditional method of cooking uses fresh, uncooked shrimp, but you can modify this with cooked shrimp for a less startling taste.

---

1 lb uncooked shrimp
1 rasher fat bacon, chopped
1 egg white, beaten lightly
1 tbsp nuoc mam
pinch of sugar
1/2 tsp black pepper

Clean and de-vein shrimp. Chop and then pound until they become a fine paste. Add chopped bacon and continue to pound until well incorporated. Blend with all other ingredients and serve as a dip (for the adventurous) or as a spread on pieces of bread to make shrimp toast.

Nuoc Leo Sauce

1/2 cup of glutinous rice
2 cups meat stock
2 cloves garlic
1 tbsp palm sugar
1 tbsp oil
4 oz minced pork
2 tbsp yellow bean sauce
1 tbsp nuoc mam
2 tbsp chili sauce
4 tbsp roasted peanuts, pounded

In a large bowl, soak glutinous rice in enough water to cover for 2 hours. Drain, bring to a boil in a large saucepan, cover, and simmer over low heat for 15 minutes until dry and set. Crush garlic and sugar together. Heat oil and fry garlic until brown. Add pork, bean sauce, *nuoc mam*, and chili sauce and simmer for 3 minutes, stirring well. Add cooked rice and simmer for 5 minutes. Stir in nuts and remove to cool before serving as a sauce with barbecue dishes.

Nem Nuong

Skewered BBQ Pork

This dish is almost like a Thai *satay* without the spices. The traditional way to make this is to pound the pork so that it can be molded around skewers. This can be labor-intensive, but the results of pounded pork and minced pork are quite different. The pork skewers are traditionally served with noodles, lettuce, mint, and *nuoc mam*.

---

1 lb leg of pork with some fat on it
2 cloves garlic, crushed
1 tbsp nuoc mam
1 tsp sugar
3 tbsp rice wine or sherry
1 tbsp ground rice
1 lb fresh rice noodles
1 small lettuce
sprigs of mint

Cut pork into pieces and pound roughly in a pestle and mortar. Add crushed garlic, *nuoc mam*, sugar, and rice wine. Add ground rice and knead mixture until it is of sausage meat consistency. Mold onto skewers (they should look like long lollipops) and barbecue or broil until brown and crusty. Drop noodles into boiling water and blanch for 1 minute, then drain and keep warm. Serve skewers on a plate with a few lettuce leaves, noodles, and mint with fish sauce on the side. Each diner assembles his or her own concoction, removing the pork from the skewers and wrapping it in a lettuce leaf. Serve with *nuoc leo* (see p. 39), a rich, meaty sauce.